interactive
SCIENCE

Dogs can hear and smell better than people can.

PEARSON

Glenview, Illinois • Boston, Massachusetts • Chandler, Arizona • Upper Saddle River, New Jersey

You are an author!

This is your own special book to keep. You can write all of your science discoveries in your book. That is why you are an author of this book.

Print your name, school, town, and state below. Then write to tell everyone all about you.

My Picture

Name

School

Town

State

All About Me

Credits appear on pages EM34–EM36, which constitute an extension of this copyright page.

ISBN-13: 978-0-328-52096-1
ISBN-10: 0-328-52096-9
15 16

On The Cover
Dogs can hear and smell better than people can.

Program Authors

DON BUCKLEY, M.Sc.
*Information and Communications Technology Director,
The School at Columbia University, New York, New York*
Mr. Buckley has been at the forefront of K–12 educational technology for nearly two decades. A founder of New York City Independent School Technologists (NYCIST) and long-time chair of New York Association of Independent Schools' annual IT conference, he has taught students on two continents and created multimedia and Internet-based instructional systems for schools worldwide.

ZIPPORAH MILLER, M.A.Ed.
Associate Executive Director for Professional Programs and Conferences, National Science Teachers Association, Arlington, Virginia
Associate executive director for professional programs and conferences at NSTA, Ms. Zipporah Miller is a former K–12 science supervisor and STEM coordinator for the Prince George's County Public School District in Maryland. She is a science education consultant who has overseen curriculum development and staff training for more than 150 district science coordinators.

MICHAEL J. PADILLA, Ph.D.
Associate Dean and Director, Eugene P. Moore School of Education, Clemson University, Clemson, South Carolina
A former middle school teacher and a leader in middle school science education, Dr. Michael Padilla has served as president of the National Science Teachers Association and as a writer of the National Science Education Standards. He is professor of science education at Clemson University. As lead author of the *Science Explorer* series, Dr. Padilla has inspired the team in developing a program that promotes student inquiry and meets the needs of today's students.

KATHRYN THORNTON, Ph.D.
Professor and Associate Dean, School of Engineering and Applied Science, University of Virginia, Charlottesville, Virginia
Selected by NASA in May 1984, Dr. Kathryn Thornton is a veteran of four space flights. She has logged over 975 hours in space, including more than 21 hours of extravehicular activity. As an author on the *Scott Foresman Science* series, Dr. Thornton's enthusiasm for science has inspired teachers around the globe.

MICHAEL E. WYSESSION, Ph.D.
Associate Professor of Earth and Planetary Science, Washington University, St. Louis, Missouri
An author on more than 50 scientific publications, Dr. Wysession was awarded the prestigious Packard Foundation Fellowship and Presidential Faculty Fellowship for his research in geophysics. Dr. Wysession is an expert on Earth's inner structure and has mapped various regions of Earth using seismic tomography. He is known internationally for his work in geoscience education and outreach.

Instructional Design Author

GRANT WIGGINS, Ed.D.
President, Authentic Education, Hopewell, New Jersey
Dr. Wiggins is a co-author with Jay McTighe of *Understanding by Design, 2nd Edition* (ASCD 2005). His approach to instructional design provides teachers with a disciplined way of thinking about curriculum design, assessment, and instruction that moves teaching from covering content to ensuring understanding.
UNDERSTANDING BY DESIGN® and UbD® are trademarks of ASCD, and are used under license.

Planet Diary Author

JACK HANKIN
Science/Mathematics Teacher, The Hilldale School, Daly City, California Founder, Planet Diary Web site
Mr. Hankin is the creator and writer of Planet Diary, a science current events website. Mr. Hankin is passionate about bringing science news and environmental awareness into classrooms.

Activities Author

KAREN L. OSTLUND, Ph.D.
Advisory Council, Texas Natural Science Center, College of Natural Sciences, The University of Texas at Austin
Dr. Ostlund has over 35 years of experience teaching at the elementary, middle school, and university levels. She was Director of WINGS Online (Welcoming Interns and Novices with Guidance and Support) and Director of the UTeach | Dell Center for New Teacher Success at the University of Texas at Austin. She served as Director of the Center for Science Education at the University of Texas at Arlington, President of the Council of Elementary Science International, and on the Board of Directors of the National Science Teachers Association. As an author of *Scott Foresman Science*, Dr. Ostlund was instrumental in developing inquiry activities.

ELL Consultant

JIM CUMMINS, Ph.D.
Professor and Canada Research Chair, Curriculum, Teaching and Learning Department at the University of Toronto
Dr. Cummins focuses on literacy development in multilingual schools and the role of technology in learning. *Interactive Science* incorporates research-based principles for integrating language with the teaching of academic content based on his work.

Reviewers

Program Consultants

William Brozo, Ph.D.
Professor of Literacy, Graduate School of Education, George Mason University, Fairfax, Virginia.
Dr. Brozo is the author of numerous articles and books on literacy development. He co-authors a column in The Reading Teacher and serves on the editorial review board of the Journal of Adolescent & Adult Literacy.

Kristi Zenchak, M.S.
Biology Instructor, Oakton Community College, Des Plaines, Illinois
Kristi Zenchak helps elementary teachers incorporate science, technology, engineering, and math activities into the classroom. STEM activities that produce viable solutions to real-world problems not only motivate students but also prepare students for future STEM careers. Ms. Zenchak helps elementary teachers understand the basic science concepts, and provides STEM activities that are easy to implement in the classroom.

Content Reviewers

Brad Armosky, M.S.
Texas Advanced Computing Center
University of Texas at Austin
Austin, Texas

Alexander Brands, Ph.D.
Department of Biological Sciences
Lehigh University
Bethlehem, Pennsylvania

Paul Beale, Ph.D.
Department of Physics
University of Colorado
Boulder, Colorado

Joy Branlund, Ph.D.
Department of Earth Science
Southwestern Illinois College
Granite City, Illinois

Constance Brown, Ph.D
Atmospheric Science Program
Geography Department
Indiana University
Bloomington, Indiana

Dana Dudle, Ph.D.
Biology Department
DePauw University
Greencastle, Indiana

Rick Duhrkopf, Ph. D.
Department of Biology
Baylor University
Waco, Texas

Mark Henriksen, Ph.D.
Physics Department
University of Maryland
Baltimore, Maryland

Andrew Hirsch, Ph.D.
Department of Physics
Purdue University
W. Lafayette, Indiana

Linda L. Cronin Jones, Ph.D.
School of Teaching & Learning
University of Florida
Gainesville, Florida

T. Griffith Jones, Ph.D.
College of Education
University of Florida
Gainesville, Florida

Candace Lutzow-Felling, Ph.D.
Director of Education
State Arboretum of Virginia & Blandy Experimental Farm
Boyce, VA 22620

Cortney V. Martin, Ph.D.
Virginia Polytechnic Institute
Blacksburg, Virginia

Sadredin Moosavi, Ph.D.
University of Massachusetts Dartmouth
Fairhaven, Massachusetts

Klaus Newmann, Ph.D.
Department of Geological Sciences
Ball State University
Muncie, Indiana

Scott M. Rochette, Ph.D.
Department of the Earth Sciences
SUNY College at Brockport
Brockport, New York

Ursula Rosauer Smedly, M.S.
Alcade Science Center
New Mexico State University
Alcade, New Mexico

Frederick W. Taylor, Ph.D.
Jackson School of Geosciences
University of Texas at Austin
Austin, Texas

The Nature of Science

This girl is collecting scientific information.

myscienceonline.com

Untamed Science
Watch the Ecogeeks as they learn about the nature of science.

Got it? 🕑 **60-Second Video**
Watch and learn about the nature of science.

Envision It!
See what you already know about the nature of science.

Science Songs
Sing about the nature of science.

Explore It! Animation
See how the key concepts about the nature of science come to life.

Chapter 2

The Design Process

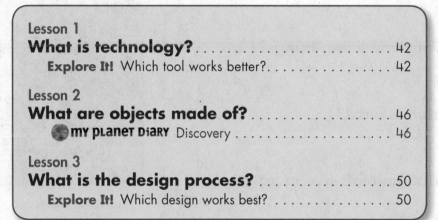

*This house for wood ducks is
made of natural materials.*

myscienceonline.com

**UntamedScience™**
Ecogeeks answer your
questions about the design
process.

Got *it?* ⏱ **60-Second Video**
Review lessons about the
design process in 60 seconds!

Memory Match
Mix and match vocabulary
practice about the design
process.

Investigate It! Simulation
Do this experiment online
to learn how you can build
a boat.

? **I Will Know...**
See what you've learned
about the design process.

Chapter 3

Living Things and Their Environments

*The beaver makes its
own shelter.*

mYscienceonLine.com

Untamed Science™
Watch the Ecogeeks in this
wild video about living things
and their environment.

Got it? ⏱ **60-Second Video**
Each living things lesson
reviewed in a minute!

Explore It! Animation
Quick and easy experiments
about living things and their
environment.

Vocabulary Smart Cards
Mix and match living things
vocabulary.

Investigate It! Simulation
Explore the needs of plants
online!

**Unit B
Summary**

Apply It! How can a mouse's color
help keep it safe from hawks? 154
Unit B
Performance-Based Assessment . . . 156

**Chapter
4**

Plants and Animals

*Salamanders live part of their
life in water and part on land.*

mYscienceonLine.com

 **Untamed Science**
Watch the Ecogeeks as they
learn about plants and
animals.

Got it? 60-Second Video
One minute videos about
every plants and animals
lesson.

Envision It!
Interact with science to find
out what you know about
plants and animals.

 **mY PLANET DIARY**
Learn fun facts about eggs.

I Will Know...
See how key concepts of each
lesson about plants and
animals are brought to life!

Unit C
Earth Science

Weathering and erosion have changed the Grand Canyon.

myscienceonline.com

 Untamed Science™
Watch the Ecogeeks learn
about Earth and sky.

Got it? 60-Second Video
Take one minute to learn
about Earth and sky.

 Science Songs
Listen to a catchy tune about
Earth and sky.

Explore It! Animation
Quick and easy experiments
about Earth and sky.

Investigate It! Simulation
Find out how rocks can crack
in this online lab.

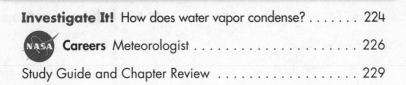

*Hurricanes have strong winds
and heavy rain.*

myscienceonline.com

Untamed Science
Watch the Ecogeeks learn
about weather.

Got it? ⏱ **60-Second Video**
Take one minute to learn
about weather.

Envision It!
Interact with science to find
out what you know about
weather.

🌎 **MY PLANET DIARY**
Learn fun facts about
seasons.

? **I Will Know...**
See how key concepts of each
lesson about weather are
brought to life!

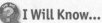

Unit D
Physical Science

Chapter 7

Matter

Matter can be a solid, liquid, or gas.

myscienceonline.com

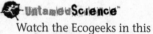
Untamed Science
Watch the Ecogeeks in this wild video about matter.

Got it? **60-Second Video**
Each matter lesson reviewed in a minute!

Explore It! **Animation**
Quick and easy experiments about matter.

Vocabulary Smart Cards
Mix and match matter vocabulary.

Investigate It! **Virtual Lab**
Find out how objects are different in this online lab.

Energy

These wind turbines use wind to make electricity.

MYSCIENCEONLINE.com

UntamedScience
Watch the Ecogeeks in this wild video about energy.

Got it? 60-Second Video
Each energy lesson reviewed in a minute!

Envision It!
See what you already know about energy.

MY PLANET DiaRY
Learn about Thomas Edison and the light bulb.

I Will Know...
See how key concepts of each lesson about energy are brought to life!

Movement

*Gravity is a force that causes
the roller coaster to go down.*

myscienceonline.com

Untamed Science
Watch the Ecogeeks in this
wild video about movement.

Got it? ⏱ **60-Second Video**
Each movement lesson
reviewed in a minute!

Memory Match
Mix and match vocabulary
practice about movement.

Explore It! Animation
Quick and easy experiments
about movement.

Investigate It! Virtual Lab
Find out how objects move in
this online lab.

Videos that bring Science to life!

Go to **MyScienceOnline.com** to watch exciting Untamed Science videos!

The Untamed Science team has created a unique video for every chapter in this book!

"This is your book. You can write in it!"

interactive SCIENCE

Big Question

At the start of each chapter you will see two questions—
an **Engaging Question** and a **Big Question.**
Just like a scientist, you will predict an answer to the
Engaging Question. Each Big Question will help you
start thinking about the Big Ideas of science. Look for the
symbol throughout the chapter!

How is a young orangutan like its mother?

Plants and Animals

Chapter 4

...one way the baby and its mother ...alike.

How are living things alike and different?

Go to www.myscienceonline.com and click on:

Untamed Science
Ecogeeks answer your questions.

Got it? 60-Second Video
Lesson reviewed in a minute!

112

113

xvi

Let's Read Science!

You will see a page like this toward the beginning of each chapter. It will show you how to use a reading skill that will help you understand what you read.

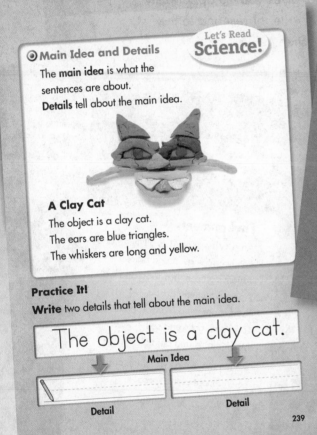

Main Idea and Details

Let's Read Science!

The **main idea** is what the sentences are about.
Details tell about the main idea.

A Clay Cat
The object is a clay cat.
The ears are blue triangles.
The whiskers are long and yellow.

Practice It!
Write two details that tell about the main idea.

The object is a clay cat.

Main Idea

Detail   Detail

239

Vocabulary Smart Cards

technology
natural
goal
solution
label

solution — solución

technology — tecnología

label — etiqueta

natural — natural

goal — objetivo

Play a Game!
Cut out the cards.
Work with a partner.
Pick a card.
Show your partner the front of the card.
Have your partner tell what the word means.

59

Vocabulary Smart Cards

Go to the end of the chapter and cut out your own set of **Vocabulary Smart Cards.** Draw a picture to learn the word. Play a game with a classmate to practice using the word!

mysclenceonLine.com   Untamed Science

Look for **MyScienceOnline.com** technology options.
At MyScienceOnline.com you can immerse yourself in virtual environments, get extra practice, and even blog about current events in science.

"Engage with the page!"

At the beginning of each lesson, at the top of the page, you will see an **Envision It!** interactivity that gives you the opportunity to circle, draw, write, or respond to the Envision It! question.

Envision It!

Lesson 3

How do plants and animals live in land environments?

Envision It!

Tell about where the horses live.

I will know how some plants and animals can live in land environments.

Words to Know

environment   prairie
forest   desert

MY PLANET DIARY Did You Know?

Read Together

Look at the bighorn sheep. Why do you think the sheep is called a bighorn?

_____

Some bighorn sheep live in deserts. They eat cactus. A cactus has sharp spines! The sheep use their big horns to scrape off the spines.

Why is this a good idea?

_____
_____
_____

Environments

An **environment** is all living and nonliving things in one place.
An environment has food and water.
An environment has air.
Land is one kind of environment.
Land has rocks and soil.
Many plants and animals live on land.

Write two things you think are in the environment of the raccoon.

_____
_____

86

87

MY PLANET DIARY

My Planet Diary interactivities will introduce you to amazing scientists, fun facts, and important discoveries in science. They will also help you to overcome common misconceptions about science concepts.

Read See DO!

After reading small chunks of information, stop to check your understanding. The visuals help teach about what you read. Answer questions, underline text, draw pictures, or label models.

Ocean Environment

An **ocean** is a large body of salty water.
Some parts of the ocean are deep.

Fish live in the ocean.
Fish have gills.
Gills let fish take in oxygen from the water.
Fish have fins.
Fins help fish swim.

Plants need sunlight to make food.
Ocean plants live where there is light.
The deep ocean is dark.
Plants do not live there.

Underline the sentence that tells how gills help fish live in the ocean.

Write why plants do not live in the deep ocean.

Draw an X on the parts of the fish that help it swim.

gills

fins

Do the math!

Tally

You can use tally marks to record information.

This is a tally mark. |

These are 5 tally marks. ||||

This chart shows how many trees are in the picture.

Living Things	Tally	Total
Tree	l	1
Bird		
Lizard		

Write tally marks to record how many birds and lizards are in the picture. Then write the totals.

Find one more living thing in the picture. **Record** the information in the chart.

Scientists commonly use math as a tool to help them answer science questions. You can practice skills that you are learning in math class right in your *Interactive Science* Student Edition!

Got it?

At the end of each chapter you will have a chance to evaluate your own progress! At this point you can stop or go on to the next chapter.

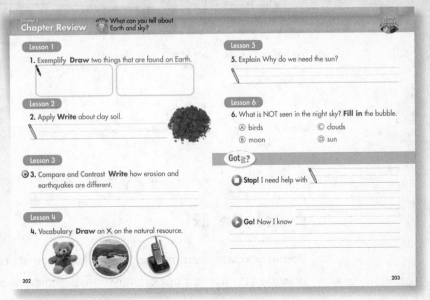

Chapter 5
Chapter Review What can you tell about Earth and sky?

Lesson 1
1. Exemplify **Draw** two things that are found on Earth.

Lesson 2
2. Apply **Write** about clay soil.

Lesson 3
3. Compare and Contrast **Write** how erosion and earthquakes are different.

Lesson 4
4. Vocabulary **Draw** an X on the natural resource.

Lesson 5
5. Explain Why do we need the sun?

Lesson 6
6. What is NOT seen in the night sky? **Fill in** the bubble.
Ⓐ birds   Ⓒ clouds
Ⓑ moon   Ⓓ sun

Got it?
Stop! I need help with

Go! Now I know

202   203

"Have fun! Be a scientist!"

interactive SCIENCE

▶ Try It!

At the start of every chapter, you will have the chance to do a hands-on inquiry activity. The activity will provide you with experiences that will prepare you for the chapter lessons or may raise a new question in your mind.

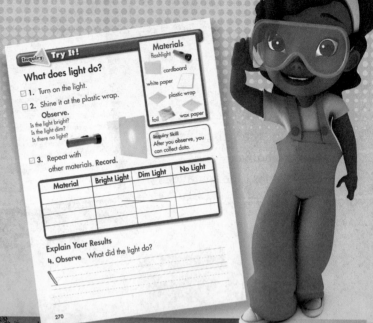

Inquiry **Try It!**

What does light do?

☐ 1. Turn on the light.

☐ 2. Shine it at the plastic wrap. **Observe.**
Is the light bright?
Is the light dim?
Is there no light?

☐ 3. Repeat with other materials. Record.

Materials
flashlight
cardboard
white paper
plastic wrap
foil   wax paper

Inquiry Skill
After you observe, you can collect data.

Material	Bright Light	Dim Light	No Light

Explain Your Results
4. **Observe** What did the light do?

270

Lesson 3
What changes land?

Envision It!

before

This volcano erupted.

after

Tell how the land changed.

I will know some fast and slow ways Earth changes.

Words to Know
weathering
erosion

Inquiry **Explore It!**

How does Earth's surface move during an earthquake?

☐ 1. Push the blocks together. Slide them past each other.

☐ 2. Push the blocks together hard. Slide them past each other.

Materials

2 sandpaper blocks

Explain Your Results

3. Did the blocks move smoothly both times? Explain.

4. **Infer** An earthquake happens (**fast/slow**). Tell why.

174

Changes on Earth

Earth is always changing. Some changes happen fast. A truck digs a hole in the ground. This is a fast change. Other changes are very slow. A river flows through land. This changes land slowly.

This truck moves rocks and soil.

Underline a way Earth can change fast.

The Colorado River makes the Grand Canyon wider and deeper.

175

▶ Explore It!

Before you start reading the lesson, **Explore It!** activities provide you with an opportunity to first explore the content!

STEM activities are found throughout core and ancillary materials.

Design It!

The **Design It!** activity has you use the engineering design process to find solutions to problems. By finding a problem and then planning, drawing, and choosing materials, you will make, test, and evaluate a solution for a real world problem. Communicate your evidence through drawings and prototypes and identify ways to make your solution better.

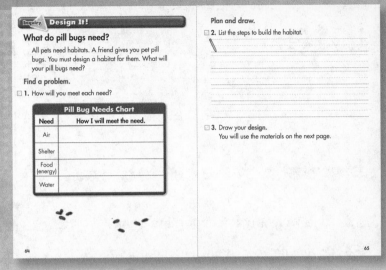

Inquiry Design It!

What do pill bugs need?

All pets need habitats. A friend gives you pet pill bugs. You must design a habitat for them. What will your pill bugs need?

Find a problem.

☐ 1. How will you meet each need?

Pill Bug Needs Chart

Need	How I will meet the need.
Air	
Shelter	
Food (energy)	
Water	

64

Plan and draw.

☐ 2. List the steps to build the habitat.

☐ 3. Draw your design.
You will use the materials on the next page.

65

Investigate It!

Inquiry Investigate It!

Do plants need light?

Follow a Procedure

☐ 1. Water both plants. Draw both plants in the chart.

Materials

2 cups with grass water

Inquiry Skill You can use a chart to record what you observe.

☐ 2. Put one cup in sunlight. Put one cup in a dark place.

☐ 3. Observe Check the plants every day. Draw both plants after 1 week.

102

Observations

Sunlight	Dark
First day	First day
After 1 week	After 1 week

Guided Inquiry

Modify Your Investigation

Investigate the Question
How might light affect the earthworms in your model ecosystem?

Open Inquiry

Design Your Own Investigation

Ask Your Own Question

At the end of every chapter, a Directed Inquiry activity gives you a chance to put together everything you've learned in the chapter. Using the activity card, apply design principles in the Guided version to Modify Your Investigation or the Open version to Develop Your Own Investigation. Whether you need a lot of support from your teacher or you're ready to explore on your own, there are fun hands-on activities that match your interests.

Apply It!

At the end of every unit, an Open Inquiry activity gives you a chance to explore science using scientific methods.

Inquiry Apply It! Using Scientific Methods

What affects how far a marble rolls?

Materials

2 metal marbles

6 books

2 metric rulers with grooves

meterstick

Inquiry Skill You control variables when you change only one thing in your test.

Ask a question.
How does ramp height affect how far a marble rolls?

Make a prediction.

1. Will a marble roll farther from a high or low ramp?
(a) high ramp
(b) low ramp

Plan a fair test.
Use two marbles that are the same.
Use two rulers that are the same.

Design your test.

☐ 2. Draw how you will set up the test.

324

☐ 3. Write your steps.

Do your test.
☐ 4. Follow your steps.

Collect and record data.
☐ 5. Fill in the chart.

Tell your conclusion.
6. Communicate How does ramp height affect how distance rolled?

325

"Go online anytime!"

interactive SCIENCE

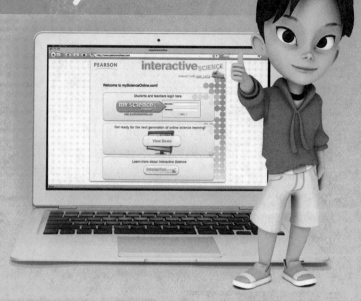

Here's how you log in...

1 Go to **www.myscienceonline.com**.

2 Log in with your username and password.

Username:

Password: _____

3 Click on your program and select your chapter.

Check it out!

Watch a Video!

Untamed Science Join the Ecogeeks on their video adventure.

Got it? 60-Second Video Review each lesson in 60 seconds.

Go Digital for Inquiry!

Explore It! Simulation Watch the lab online.

Investigate It! Virtual Lab Do the lab online.

Show What You Know!

Got it? Quiz Take a quick quiz and get instant feedback.

Benchmark Practice Prepare for the "big test."

Writing for Science Write to help you unlock the Big Question.

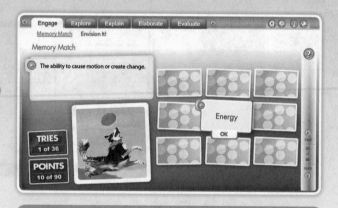

Get Excited About Science!

The Big Question Share what you think about the Big Question.

my planet diary Connect to the world of science.

Envision It! Connect to what you already know before you start each lesson.

Memory Match Play a game to build your vocabulary.

Get Help!

my science coach Get help at your level.

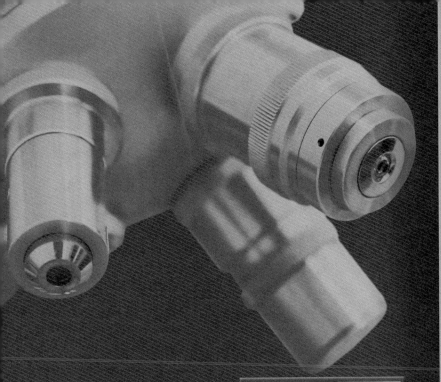

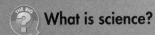

How are you a **scientist** when you bake?

The Nature of Science

Try It! How do you use your senses to identify objects?

Lesson 1 What questions do scientists ask?

Lesson 2 What skills do scientists use?

Lesson 3 How do scientists use tools?

Lesson 4 How do scientists find answers?

Lesson 5 How do scientists share data?

Investigate It! How do you know the mass of objects?

Circle a tool bakers use.

 What is science?

Go to www.myscienceonline.com and click on:

Untamed Science
Watch the Ecogeeks in this wild video.

Got it? **60-Second Video**
Review each lesson in 60 seconds!

How do you use your senses to identify objects?

Materials

sock with object   crayons

Scientists observe to find out about objects.

☐ **1. Observe**   Feel the object in the sock. Do not look!

☐ **2. Record** what it feels like.

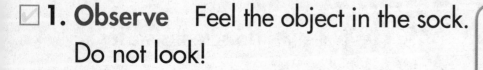

☐ **3. Infer**   Draw the object.

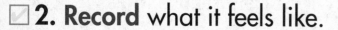

Explain Your Results

4. Look at the object.
   What do you see that you did not feel?

◉ Picture Clues

Pictures can give you **clues** about what you read.

At the Vet

The dog is at the vet.
The vet helps the dog stay healthy.

Practice It!

Look for clues in the picture. **Write** how you know the dog stays healthy.

At the Vet

The dog is at the vet.

Clue

Clue

5

What questions do scientists ask?

Tell what a scientist might ask about the leaves.

MY PLANET DIARY   DISCOVERY

Read Together

George Washington Carver discovered new ways to make things with plant parts. He made ink, shampoo, soap, paper, and rubber from peanuts!

Sometimes people like George Washington Carver are looking for new things. Sometimes people discover new things by accident. Discoveries help people do things they could not do before.

Circle one thing George Washington Carver made in a new way.

Write how you use this discovery.

Word to Know

inquiry

Scientists

Scientists are people who study the world around them.

Scientists ask and answer questions.

Scientists use inquiry.

Inquiry means looking for answers.

The boy is a scientist. He is studying what is in the jar.

◉ **Picture Clues** **Write** two questions the boy in the picture might ask.

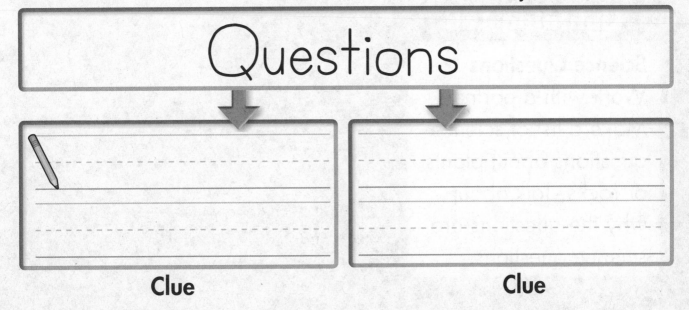

Questions

Clue   Clue

7

Questions

Scientists ask questions about many things.

Scientists ask questions about animals.

Scientists ask questions about plants.

Scientists ask questions about rocks and soil.

Scientists ask questions about weather too.

Write a question you might ask about this storm.

_____

_____

_____

Lightning Lab

Science Questions

Work with a partner. Make a list of science questions about plants or rocks. Talk about why the questions are science questions.

Discovery

Scientists make discoveries.
A discovery is a new thing or idea.
Discoveries can change our lives.
The discovery of germs changed
the way people act.
Doctors did not always wash their hands
with soap.
People would get germs from the doctor.
Now doctors wash their hands with soap.
The soap gets rid of germs.
Their tools are washed with soap too.
Doctors do not pass germs to others.

Name one discovery. **Tell** how it
helped people.

9

Lesson 2

What skills do scientists use?

Tell about the picture. Use your senses.

Inquiry **Explore It!**

How can you observe objects?

Materials

feather

crayons or markers

hand lens

☑ **1.** Look at a feather.

Observe it with a hand lens.

Draw what you see.

☑ **2.** Feel the feather. Tell what you learn.

Explain Your Results

3. How did the hand lens help you **observe**?

10

UNLOCK THE BIG ? I will know skills scientists use to learn about new things.

Word to Know

observe

The Five Senses

You **observe** when you use your senses.

You have five senses.

Your senses are sight, hearing, smell, touch, and taste.

You can observe color with your sense of sight.

You can observe size and shape with your senses of sight and touch.

This tree frog lives in the rainforest.

Underline the sentence that tells how you observe.

◉ Picture Clues **Write** one thing you observe about the frog in the picture.

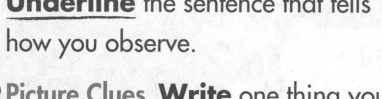

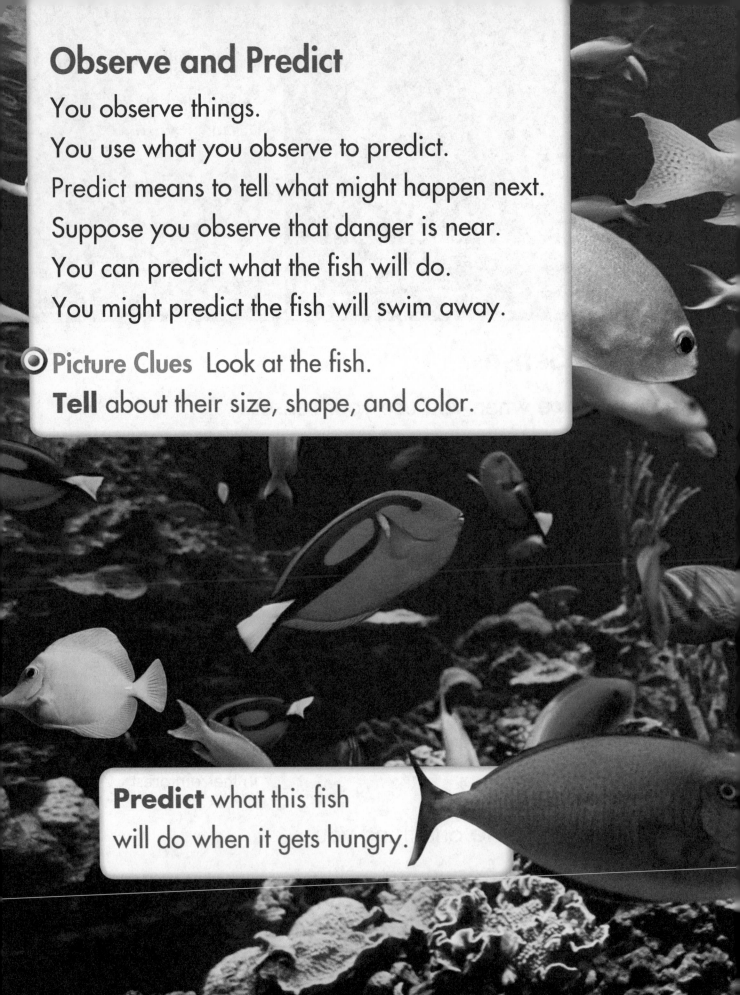

Observe and Predict

You observe things.

You use what you observe to predict.

Predict means to tell what might happen next.

Suppose you observe that danger is near.

You can predict what the fish will do.

You might predict the fish will swim away.

⊙ **Picture Clues** Look at the fish.

Tell about their size, shape, and color.

Predict what this fish
will do when it gets hungry.

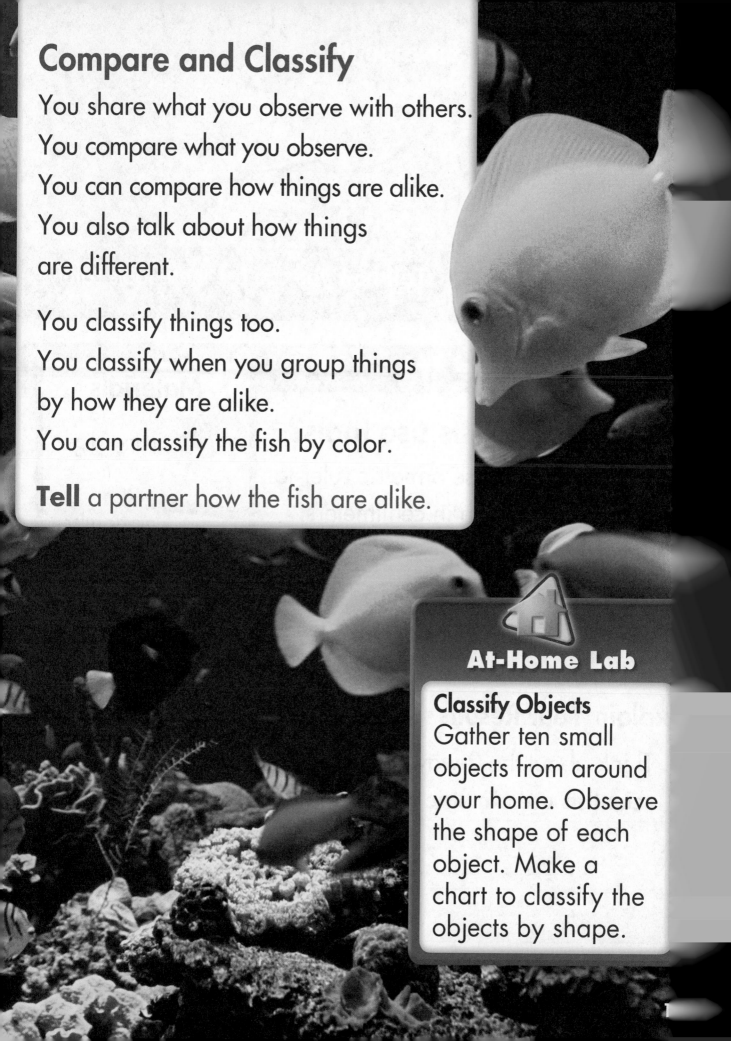

Compare and Classify

You share what you observe with others.
You compare what you observe.
You can compare how things are alike.
You also talk about how things
are different.

You classify things too.
You classify when you group things
by how they are alike.
You can classify the fish by color.

Tell a partner how the fish are alike.

At-Home Lab

Classify Objects
Gather ten small
objects from around
your home. Observe
the shape of each
object. Make a
chart to classify the
objects by shape.

How do scientists use tools?

Tell how you can use these tools safely.

Inquiry | **Explore It!**

Why do scientists use tools?

☐ **1.** Pick an object. Use a metric ruler to **measure** its length in centimeters. **Record**.

☐ **2.** Use paper clips to measure the object. Record its length in paper clips.

Explain Your Results

3. Think about the 2 ways you **measured**. Why might scientists use a metric ruler and not paper clips?

_____

_____

_____

Materials

paper clips

metric ruler

Object Length

Length in centimeters	
Length in paper clips	

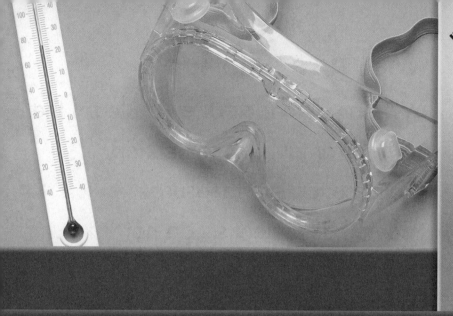

UNLOCK THE BIG ?

I will know how to use some science tools. I will know how to do science safely.

Words to Know

tool   safety

measure

Tools

Scientists use many different tools.

A **tool** is something that makes work easier.

You can use tools to observe.

A hand lens is a tool.

A hand lens makes objects look bigger.

A microscope makes objects look bigger too.

You can see small things with a microscope.

You cannot see these things with just your eyes.

<u>**Underline**</u> what makes work easier.

Draw an X on the tool that helps you see things you cannot see with just your eyes.

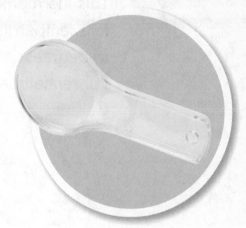

hand lens

microscope

15

A **thermometer** measures temperature. Temperature is how hot or cold something is. This thermometer tells temperature in degrees Fahrenheit and Celsius.

Measure with Tools

When you **measure** you learn the size or amount of something.

You use tools to measure.

Sometimes scientists do not measure.

Sometimes scientists estimate.

An estimate is a careful guess about the size or amount of something.

Circle the tool that measures how hot something is.

A **rain gauge** measures how much rain has fallen.

Lightning Lab

Measure Temperature
Use a thermometer. Measure the temperature in your classroom. Tell the temperature in degrees Fahrenheit and Celsius.

A **pan balance** measures how much mass an object has.

A **clock** measures time.

A **measuring cup** measures volume. Volume is how much space something takes up.

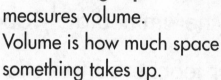

A **ruler** measures how long something is. This ruler measures in inches and centimeters.

Choose a tool to measure how long your shoe is.
Write what it measures in inches and centimeters.

Safety in Science

Safety means staying out of danger.
Follow these safety rules when you do activities.

1. Never taste or smell materials unless told to do so.

2. Keep your workplace neat and clean.

3. Tell your teacher immediately about accidents.

4. Listen to your teacher's instructions.

5. Wash your hands well after each activity.

Write another rule for the chart.

The girl washes her hands with soap and water.

Picture Clues **Tell** how the girl stays safe.

Tie your hair back if it is long.

Wear safety goggles when needed.

Wear gloves to keep your hands safe.

Handle scissors and other equipment carefully.

Clean up spills immediately.

You spill water on the floor.

Circle the rule that you should follow.

Write why it is important to follow safety rules.

19

How do scientists find answers?

Envision It!

Tell what the person might want to learn.

 **Explore It!**

How do scientists answer questions?

☑ Think about the following question.
Can sunlight warm an object?

Answer the question as a scientist would.

Materials

black paper

☑ **1. Observe** a piece of paper. Feel it. It is **(warm/cool).**

☑ **2.** Make a **prediction.**
The paper will get **(warm/cool)** in sunlight.

☑ **3.** Test your prediction. Put the paper in sunlight.
Wait 15 minutes. The paper got **(warm/cool)**.

Explain Your Results

4. Draw a Conclusion Can sunlight warm objects?
Tell how you know.

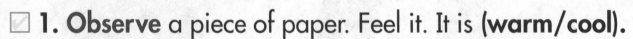

Word to Know

investigate

Science Inquiry

You ask questions when you do science.
You investigate to find answers.
To **investigate** is to look for answers
to questions.

Scientific methods are a way
to investigate.
Scientific methods have many steps.

This scientist
investigates plants.

(Circle) the word that means to look
for answers to questions.

◎ **Picture Clues** Look at the picture.
Ask a question the scientist might ask
about plants.

Scientific Methods

Ask a question.

Ask a question that you want answered. *How does sunlight change the way plants grow?*

Make your hypothesis.

Tell what you think might be the answer to your question.

If a plant is moved away from sunlight, then it will grow toward the sunlight because plants need light.

Plan a fair test.

Change only one thing. Keep everything else the same. *Move one plant away from the window.*

Tell another hypothesis.

Do your test.

Test your hypothesis.

Do your test more than once.

Observe the results of your test.

See if your results are the same.

Collect and record your data.

Keep records of what you find.

Use words or drawings to help.

Draw a conclusion.

Decide if your observations
match your hypothesis.

Tell what you decide.

Compare your conclusion
with a partner's conclusion.

Lightning Lab

Fast Claps

How many times can
you clap your hands
in one minute? Plan a
test with three steps.
Do your test.

The boy draws a picture to
keep records.

○ **Picture Clues** **Write** how sunlight
changes the way plants grow.

_____

_____

_____

Tell how you know.

How do scientists share data?

Envision It!

Write what you observe about the dog.

What are some ways to record and share data?

☑ **1.** Stack the cups as high as you can. Make a tally mark each time you add a cup.

☑ **2.** **Record** the total using a number.

☑ **3.** Repeat 3 more times.

Explain Your Results

4. Compare data with others. Tell any pattern you find.

5. You **recorded data** in 2 ways. How else could you have recorded data?

Materials

10 paper cups

Trial	Number of Cups	Total
1		
2		
3		
4		

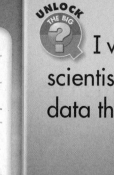

UNLOCK THE BIG ? I will know how scientists share the data they collect.

Words to Know

data   record

Data

You collect information when you do science.

This information is called **data.**

You can use pictures and words to show what you observe.

You can use numbers too.

◉ **Picture Clues Draw** the data that the girl in the picture might draw.

25

Record Data

You **record** when you write
or draw what you learn.
A chart is a way to record data.

Ask five people if they like a cat, a
dog, or a bird best.
Fill in a square in the chart next to
the animals your classmates choose.

Favorite Animals

cat					
dog					
bird					

At-Home Lab

Favorite Pet Name
Think of three pet
names. Ask six people
which name they like
best. Make a chart to
record their choices.

Show Data

You can use charts to show data.
You can also use graphs.
Use your data to make a
picture graph.

Count the votes for each pet.
Draw one animal for each vote.

Favorite Animals

Pet		1	2	3	4	5
	cat					
	dog					
	bird					

Number of votes

Write a conclusion from your data.

27

How do you know the mass of objects?

Follow a Procedure

☑ **1. Measure** the mass of a cup.
First, put the cup on one side of a balance.
Next, slowly add gram cubes to the other side.
Then, stop when the balance is level.
Last, **record** the mass on the chart.

☑ **2.** Measure the mass of 10 beans. Record.

☑ **3.** Measure the mass of the cup with the 10 beans inside. Record.

Materials

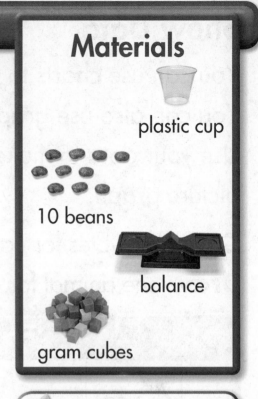

plastic cup

10 beans

balance

gram cubes

Inquiry Skill Scientists observe what happens and **record** their results.

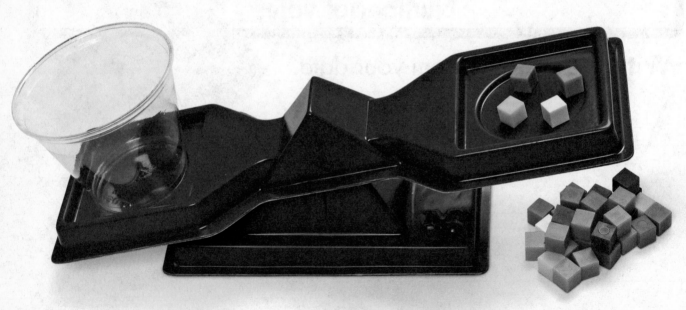

Mass of Objects

Object	Mass (grams)
Cup	
10 beans	
Cup with 10 beans	

Analyze and Conclude

4. Look at your data.
   Add the mass of the cup and the beans.

   _____ grams + _____ grams = _____ grams
   (cup)   (beans)   (cup with 10 beans)

5. **Draw a Conclusion**   Did the cup and beans have the same mass together as they did separately?

   _____

   _____

   _____

Big World

Hubble Space Telescope

Look up at the night sky. The stars seem to twinkle. They twinkle because of the air around Earth. The air blocks our clear view of the stars. The Hubble Space Telescope circles above Earth's air. It has a clear view of the stars and other things in space. The telescope sends pictures to Earth. Scientists use the pictures to study space.

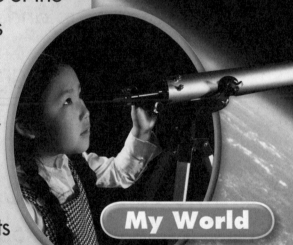

My World

Write how the Hubble Space Telescope helps scientists study space.

Vocabulary Smart Cards

inquiry
observe
tool
measure
safety
investigate
data
record

Play a Game!

Cut out the cards.

Work with a partner.

Pick a card.

Act out the word.

Have your partner guess the word.

measure

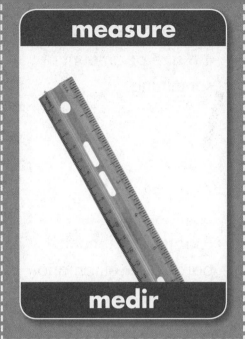

medir

inquiry

indagación

safety

seguridad

observe

observar

investigate

investigar

tool

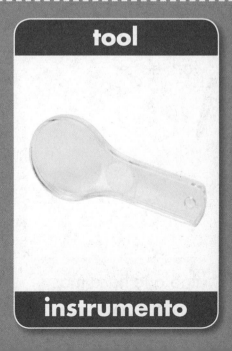

instrumento

looking for answers

buscar respuestas

to use a tool to find the size or amount of something

usar un instrumento para saber el tamaño o la cantidad de algo

when you use your senses

cuando usas tus sentidos

staying out of danger

estar fuera de peligro

something that makes work easier

algo que hace más fácil el trabajo

to look for answers to questions

buscar respuestas a las preguntas

data

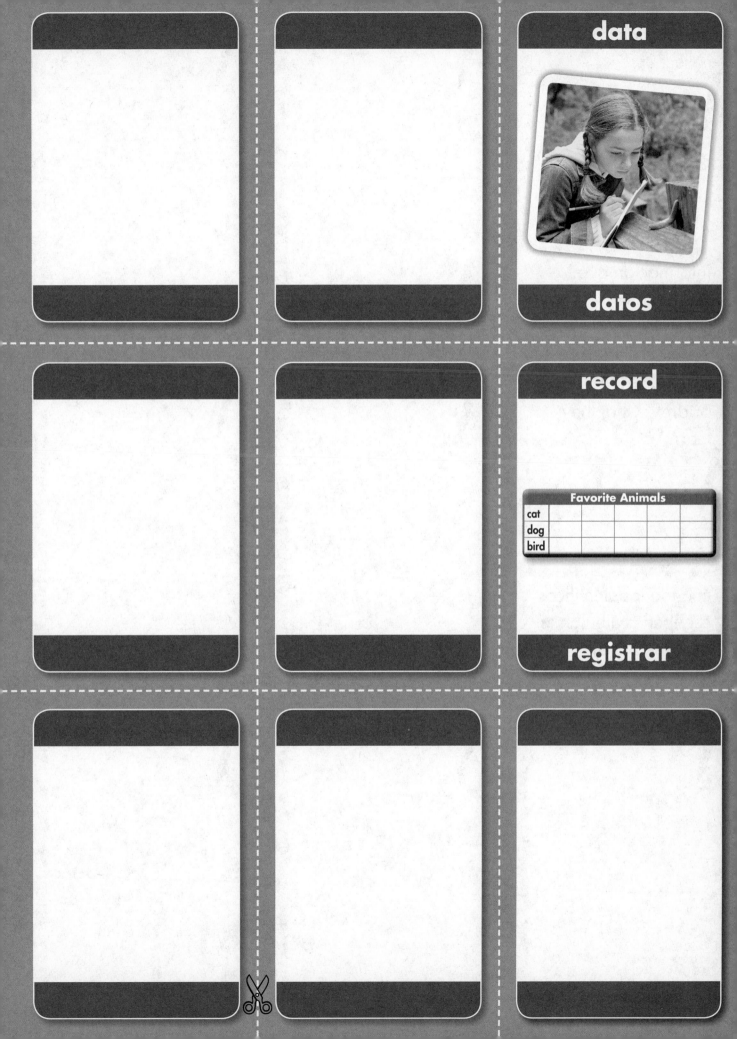

datos

record

Favorite Animals				
cat				
dog				
bird				

registrar

information you
collect

información que
reúnes

when scientists write
or draw what they
learn

cuando los científicos
escriben o dibujan lo
que descubren

Lesson 1 What questions do scientists ask?
- Scientists ask questions about the world.
- Scientists answer questions with inquiry.

Lesson 2 What skills do scientists use?
- Scientists use their senses to observe.
- Your senses help you describe things.

Lesson 3 How do scientists use tools?
- You can use tools to measure objects.
- Always follow safety rules.

Lesson 4 How do scientists find answers?
- Scientists use many methods to investigate.
- Scientists test things many times.

Lesson 5 How do scientists share data?
- Scientists observe and record data.
- You can use charts to record.

Chapter Review

REVIEW THE BIG ❓ What is science?

Lesson 1

1. Vocabulary What is inquiry?

_____

_____

2. Apply Some scientists ask questions about weather. **Write** a question you have about weather.

_____

_____

_____

Lesson 2

3. Compare (Circle) the scientist who listens to observe.

Lesson 3

4. Picture Clues **Write** how the children stay safe.

_____

_____

Lesson 4

5. Vocabulary Write what scientists do when
they investigate.

_____

‗ ‗

Lesson 5

6. What do scientists use to keep records? **Fill in** the bubble.

Ⓐ words and pictures   Ⓒ safety

Ⓑ tools such as saws   Ⓓ scientific methods

Got it?

▢ **Stop!** I need help with _____

_____

‗ ‗

▶ Go! Now I know _____

_____

‗ ‗

What are they
making?

The Design Process

Try It! How can you design a top?

Lesson 1 What is technology?

Lesson 2 What are objects made of?

Lesson 3 What is the design process?

Investigate It! How can you build a boat?

Write what you think they will make.

_____

How do you solve problems?

Go to www.myscienceonline.com and click on:

UntamedScience™
Ecogeeks answer your questions.

Got it? 60-Second Video
Everything you learned in 60 seconds

my planet Diary
Learn about new discoveries.

Investigate It! Simulation
Quick and easy online experiments

How can you design a top?

☑ **1.** Make the top in the picture.

Materials

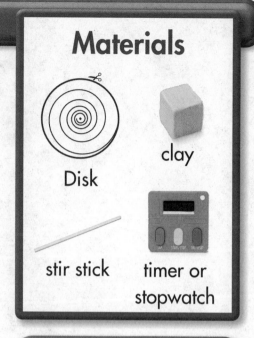

Disk

clay

stir stick

timer or stopwatch

☑ **2. Measure** Test your top.
How long did it spin? **Record.**

☑ **3. Redesign** your top to spin longer.
Draw and label your **design.**

Inquiry Skill
You can use what you observe to **infer.**

Time (seconds)

First top	
Second top	

☑ **4.** Make your new top. Repeat Step 2.

Explain Your Results

5. Infer Why did one top spin longer?

⦿ Sequence

Sequence means to tell what happens first, next, and last.

Block Castle

You want to build a block castle.
First, you gather blocks.
Next, you stack the blocks.
Last, you look at your castle.
It is very high!

Practice It!

Write what comes next.

First

I gather blocks.

↓

Next

↓

Last

I look at my castle.

What is technology?

Write the parts of the bicycle.
Use words from the list.

Inquiry Explore It!

Which tool works better?

☑ **1. Predict**   Which tool will pick up cubes better?

☑ **2.** Use each tool to pick up cubes.

Explain Your Results

3. Record   What happened when you used each tool?

_____

4. Draw a Conclusion   Which tool worked better? Explain.

_____

_____

Materials

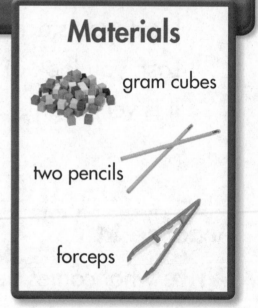

gram cubes

two pencils

forceps

tire
pedal
seat
handlebars

Technology

Bicycles are a kind of technology.
Technology is using science to help solve problems.
Scientists use technology to make discoveries.
Sometimes scientists discover new technology.

Technology helps scientists do their work.

(Circle) the technology the boy is using.

Tell what it is.

Tell what would happen if a bicycle did not have one of its pedals.

Helping Earth
Think of a technology that helps keep the air or water clean. Tell how it helps.

This boy uses a pencil to communicate. A pencil is technology.

Solve Problems

Technology helps people solve problems.

One problem is that people need to communicate with each other. They might not be in the same place.

They use a telephone.

A telephone is technology.

Underline a problem that technology solves.

◉ Sequence **Look** at the time line. **Write** what people invented first.

Technology over Time

1870

The first all metal bicycle is invented.

1876

The first telephone call is made.

1946

The first computer is built.

Help People

Technology helps people stay safe.

People use cars to get from place to place.

Seat belts help make cars safe.

Air bags help make cars safe.

Safety seats help keep children safe.

Technology helps keep people safe in cars.

Underline three kinds of technology a car has.

Draw another kind of technology.

Tell how it solves a problem or helps people.

2001

MP3 players become popular.

Draw something you would like to invent.

Tell three objects that people made.

MY PLANET DIARY

DISCOVERY

Do you like to eat popcorn? Orville Redenbacher wanted to find the kind of corn that made the best popcorn. He grew many different kinds of popcorn. He tested many kinds of corn. Finally, he found a corn that made good popcorn.

Underline what Orville Redenbacher tested.

Write something you would like to test.

Word to Know

natural

Different Materials

Objects are made of materials.

Some materials are natural.

Natural means not made by people.

Materials that come directly from
Earth are natural.

Wood and cotton are natural.

Rocks and minerals are natural too.

Sometimes people use natural
materials to make new materials.

Plastic is a new material people make.

Write one natural material and one
material made by people in the picture.

Natural Materials

Natural materials are
different from each other.

They can be used in different ways.
Wood is hard.
People use wood to make buildings.
Cotton is soft.
People use cotton to make clothes.

Circle the kind of material you
might use to make a pillow.
Tell why you might use that material.

⦿ **Picture Clues**
Write why you think
rock is a good material
for building a house.

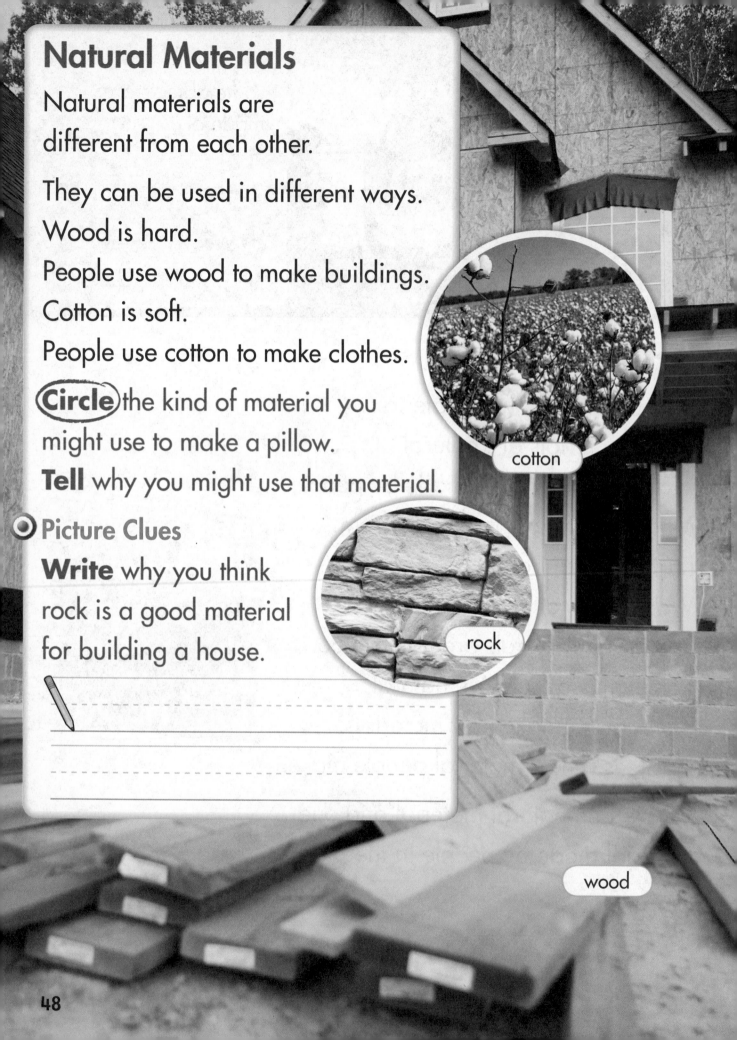

cotton

rock

wood

Man-Made Materials

People make new materials.
These new materials can be used in different ways.

Plastic is a new material.
Some plastic is hard.
Some plastic is soft.

Some objects are made of more than one material.
A chair can be made of plastic and wood.

Write two things that are made of plastic.

People store food in plastic containers.

Packing foam is made by people.

At-Home Lab

Materials
Find two objects.
Tell what materials the objects are made of.
Tell if the materials are natural or made by people.

What is the design process?

Draw a line from the bowl to each object that might be inside.

Inquiry Explore It!

Which design works best?

 1. Pick a bird feeder to build.

 2. Build it. Put it outside.

 3. Observe for 5 days. **Record.**
Compare your feeder with others.

Explain Your Results

4. Which **design** worked the best?

_____

5. How can you **redesign** your feeder to attract more birds?

_____

Materials

Bird Feeder Chart

Build a Bird Feeder

binder clips

bird feeder food

scissors

string   containers

Words to Know

goal   solution

A Problem and a Goal

Wood ducks are animals that need shelter.

This is a problem.

You want to help wood ducks find shelter.

First, you set a goal to design a house for wood ducks.

A **goal** is something you want to do.

Your wood duck house will be a solution.

A **solution** solves a problem.

(Circle) the problem.

Underline the goal.

Wood ducks do not make their own shelter. They use shelters made by people or other animals.

51

Plan and Draw

Next, you make a plan to build your house for wood ducks.

You write about how to make your house for wood ducks.

You draw what your house for wood ducks will look like.

○ **Sequence** First, you set a goal.

Write what you will do next.

_____

_____

_____

Draw what your house for wood ducks will look like.

Choose Materials

Next, you decide what materials to use
to make your house for wood ducks.
You choose something for the walls.
You might choose wood.
You choose something to hold
the walls together.
You might choose nails.
You need something on the inside so
the wood ducks can climb out.
You might choose a piece of screen.

(Circle) three things you need to make
the house for wood ducks.

tape

wood

screen

nails

microphone

Wood ducks live in many parts of the Midwest and Eastern United States.

Make and Test

Next, you make your house for wood ducks.

You decide where to put it.

You test the house.

You check the house every day.

You see if wood ducks live there.

Write how you know a house for wood ducks works well.

You can share your solution with other people.

Record and Share

You decide how well your solution works.

You plan again to make your solution better.

Next, you record your new plan.

You write and draw to tell about your solution.

You use labels to show parts of your solution.

A label shows what something is.

This helps you remember what you learn.

You can use your solution again.

Last, you can show others how your solution meets your goal.

Label the details of the house for wood ducks.

⊙ Sequence **Tell** the sequence you can use to build a house for wood ducks. Use the words first, next, and last.

How can you build a boat?

In this activity you will build a **model** of a boat using foil.

Follow a Procedure

☐ **1. Design** a boat that will float. Draw your design.

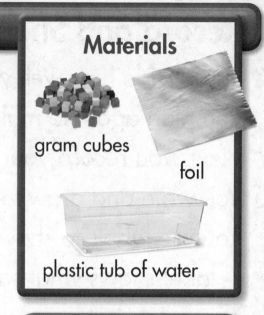

Materials

gram cubes

foil

plastic tub of water

Inquiry Skill
When you **predict**, you tell what you think might happen.

☐ **2.** Build your boat. Test it in the tub of water.

☑ **3.** Add gram cubes to your boat until it sinks. **Record.**

☑ **4. Redesign** your boat to hold more cubes. **Predict** how many gram cubes it will hold before it sinks. Record.

☑ **5.** Test your prediction. Add cubes to your boat until it sinks. Record.

Analyze and Conclude

6. Draw a Conclusion Did your boat hold more or less cubes than your **prediction**?

_____

_____

_____

_____

7. **UNLOCK THE BIG ?** How did you **redesign** your boat to hold more gram cubes?

_____

_____

_____

_____

Science
Technology
Engineering
Math

STEM

Read Together

Trains

When was the last time you rode in a train? Trains are a kind of transportation. Transportation helps us move from place to place.

Technology has changed trains. Engineers design trains. Engineers use technology to make trains move faster. They use technology to make trains safer.

The first trains were powered by steam. Today some bullet trains are powered by electricity. Some trains can travel over 300 kph.

Cars are also a type of transportation. How do you think cars have changed the way we move?

_____

_____

_____

Vocabulary Smart Cards

technology
natural
goal
solution

Play a Game!

Cut out the cards.

Work with a partner.

Pick a card.

Show your partner the front of the card.

Have your partner tell what the word means.

solution

solución

technology

tecnología

natural

natural

goal

objetivo

using science to help solve problems

usar las ciencias para resolver problemas

something that solves a problem

algo que resuelve un problema

not made by people

no hecho por las personas

something you want to do

algo que quieres hacer

Chapter 2
Study Guide

REVIEW THE BIG ? How do you solve problems?

Science,
Engineering,
and
Technology

Lesson 1

What is technology?
- Technology is any tool that helps people.
- People use technology to solve problems.

Lesson 2

What are objects made of?
- Materials not made by people are natural.
- People use materials for different things.

Lesson 3

What is the design process?
- Something you want to do is a goal.
- You can record your solution with labels.

Lesson 1

1. **Vocabulary** Put an ✗ on a kind of technology.

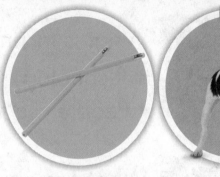

2. **Apply** Technology helps solve problems. **Write** a problem you would like to solve.

_____

_____

_____

Lesson 2

3. **Sort** (Circle) the object with no natural materials.

4. **Describe** **Write** an object that has natural materials and materials made by people.

_____

_____

_____

Lesson 3

⊙ **5. Sequence Write** what you do first to solve a problem.

_____

_____

6. How could you test a new ant farm? **Fill in** the bubble.

Ⓐ put food inside   Ⓒ draw the ant farm

Ⓑ tell about the ant farm   Ⓓ see if ants will live there

Got it?

☐ **Stop!** I need help with _____

_____

_____

▶ **Go!** Now I know _____

_____

_____

What do pill bugs need?

All pets need habitats. A friend gives you pet pill bugs. You must design a habitat for them. What will your pill bugs need?

Find a problem.

☑ **1.** How will you meet each need?

Pill Bug Needs Chart

Need	How I will meet the need.
Air	
Shelter	
Food (energy)	
Water	

Plan and draw.

☑ **2.** List the steps to build the habitat.

_____

- -

_____

_____

- -

_____

_____

- -

_____

_____

- -

_____

☑ **3.** Draw your **design.**
You will use the materials on the next page.

Choose materials.

☑ **4.** Circle the materials you will use.

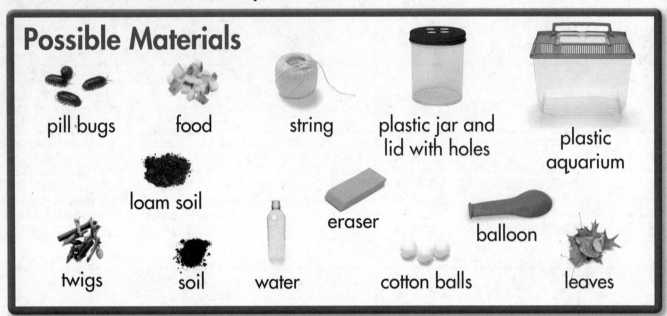

Possible Materials

pill bugs　　food　　string　　plastic jar and lid with holes　　plastic aquarium

loam soil

eraser　　balloon

twigs　　soil　　water　　cotton balls　　leaves

☑ **5.** Tell which need each material meets.

Make and test.

☑ **6.** Make the habitat you **designed.**
Follow your plan.

☑ **7.** Draw your pill bugs in the habitat.

Record and share.

☑ **8. Observe** your design for one week.
Observe the habitat.
Observe the pill bugs.

Day	Observation
Day Observations	
1	
2	
3	
4	
5	

These pill bugs are shown
five times their regular size.

9. Compare your habitat with other groups.
How were the habitats the same?

10. How were the habitats different?

11. How could you **redesign** your pill bug habitat?

Design a New Hat

- Design a new hat.

- Draw a picture of the hat. Label parts of the hat.

- Tell about your picture.

Write a Poem

- Think of a goal.

- Write a poem about a solution for your goal.

Test Materials

- Draw lines with a pen, a marker, and a crayon.

- Use an eraser to erase your lines.

- Write a sentence about which material erases best.

Using Scientific Methods

1. Ask a question.

2. Make a hypothesis.

3. Plan a fair test.

4. Do your test.

5. Collect and record data.

6. Tell your conclusion.

Life Science

Where does a cow get food?

Living Things and Their Environments

 Try It! What does a cricket need?

Lesson 1 What are nonliving and living things?

Lesson 2 What do living things need?

Lesson 3 How do plants and animals live in land environments?

Lesson 4 How do plants and animals live in water environments?

Lesson 5 What plants and animals no longer live on Earth?

Investigate It! Do plants need light?

Draw an ✗ on one thing a cow needs.

 What do plants and animals need?

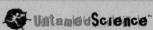
Go to www.myscienceonline.com and click on: ⊗

Untamed Science™
Ecogeeks answer your questions.

Got it? 60-Second Video
Watch and learn.

What does a cricket need?

☐ **1. Observe** the cricket each day.

Materials

cricket in habitat

Inquiry Skill
You **observe** when you watch living things in their environment.

☐ **2.** What did the cricket do? Record what you see with an X.

Cricket Observations

Day	Eats	Drinks	Moves Around	Hides or Sleeps
1				
2				
3				
4				

Explain Your Results

3. Tell what the cricket needs. Use your **observations**.

_____

_____

_____

_____

◉ **Draw Conclusions**

You **draw conclusions** when you decide something about what you see and read.

Animals Underwater

Many animals live in the water.
Fish and coral might live here.
The animals get what they need in the water.

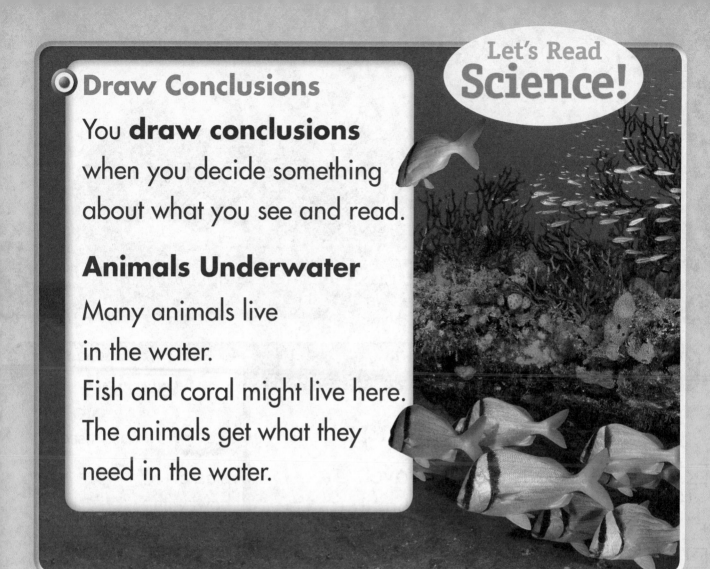

Practice It!

Write a conclusion about where fish get what they need.

I know

Fish live in water.

My conclusion

What are nonliving and living things?

Envision It!

Draw one more object in the fish tank.

 **Explore It!**

Which is a living thing?

☐ **1.** Put the seeds on the gravel.
Barely cover the gravel with water.

☐ **2. Record** your **observations.**

Materials

bean seeds

plastic bowl with gravel

plastic cup with water

Daily Observations

Day 1	
Day 2	
Day 3	
Day 4	

Explain Your Results

3. Infer Which is living? Explain. _____

_____

_____

I will know how nonliving things are different from living things.

Words to Know

nonliving
living

Tell if it is living or nonliving.

Nonliving Things

Nonliving things do not grow.
Nonliving things do not change on their own.
Nonliving things do not have young.
Nonliving things do not move on their own.

Write two nonliving things that are in the toy box.
Tell why they are nonliving.

Living Things

Living things can grow.

Living things can change on their own.

Living things can have young.

Many living things move on their own.

Plants are living things.

Animals are living things.

You are a living thing too.

Look at the picture.
(Circle) two living things.
Draw an X on two nonliving things.

◉ Draw a Conclusion **Tell** how you know which things are living.

At-Home Lab

Living and Nonliving

List some living things in your home. List some nonliving things. Make a chart. Tell how you know whether each thing is living or nonliving.

What do living things need?

water

and

soil

and

Draw what you think the grown plant will look like.

Inquiry **Explore It!**

Do plants need water?

☐ **1. Observe** the plant. Add water.

☐ **2. Predict** what will happen.

_____

- -

_____

☐ **3.** Wait 1 day. **Record** your observation.

_____

- -

_____

- -

_____

Materials

plant   water

Explain Your Results

4. Predict What will happen if you do not water the plant?

_____

- -

_____

UNLOCK THE BIG ?

I will know that living things need air, water, food, and space.

Words to Know

need   shelter
nutrients

Needs

All living things have needs.
A **need** is something a living thing must have to live.
Plants and animals are living things.
Plants and animals have needs.
People have needs too.

Poppy plants have needs.

⊙ Draw a **conclusion** about the needs of the poppy plants in the picture.

I know

The poppy plants are living.

My conclusion

Needs of Plants

Plants need air.

Plants need water.

Plants need light to make food.

Plants need space to live and grow.

Tell how you know the strawberry plants get what they need.

Draw one thing the strawberry plants need.

strawberry plants

Nutrients

Plants need nutrients.

Nutrients are materials
that living things need.
Plants can get nutrients from the soil.

Point to where the strawberry
plants get nutrients. **Write** why the
strawberry plants need nutrients.

Lightning Lab

Play a Plant
Sit on the floor. Raise
both hands. You are
a plant. You get no
water. Slowly show
what happens.

Needs of Animals

Animals need air and water.

Animals need food.

Animals get nutrients from food.

Animals need space to live.

Some animals need shelter.

Shelter is a safe place.

Beavers build their
own shelter.

Write how the needs of plants
and animals are different.

Needs of People

People need air and water.

People need food.

People get nutrients from food.

People need space to live.

People need shelter.

Shelter keeps people warm and dry.

◉ Draw Conclusions **Write** how shelter helps some people in winter.

_____

_____

Tell what this family needs.

Vitamin D is a nutrient in milk.

How do plants and animals live in land environments?

Tell about where the horses live.

my planet diary Did You Know?

Look at the bighorn sheep.
Why do you think the sheep is
called a bighorn?

_____

_____

Some bighorn sheep live in deserts.
They eat cactus. A cactus has sharp
spines! The sheep use their big
horns to scrape off the spines.

Why is this a good idea?

_____

_____

_____

UNLOCK THE BIG ?

I will know how some plants and animals can live in land environments.

Words to Know

environment   prairie
forest   desert

Environments

An **environment** is all living and
nonliving things in one place.

An environment has food and water.

An environment has air.

Land is one kind of environment.

Land has rocks and soil.

Many plants and animals live on land.

Write two things you think are in the
environment of the raccoon.

Forest Environment

A forest is a land environment.
A **forest** is land that has
many trees and other plants.

Black bears live in some forests.
Black bears have sharp claws.
Bears use their claws to dig for food.
Sharp claws help bears climb trees.

◉ Draw a Conclusion **Tell** why the
bear in the picture might have
climbed a tree.

Big leaves help forest plants
take in a lot of sunlight.

Prairie Environment

A prairie is a land environment.

A **prairie** is flat land that is covered with grasses.

Prairie dogs live in some prairies.

Prairie dogs have sharp teeth.

Sharp teeth help them chew the prairie grass.

Prairie dogs have sharp claws.

Sharp claws help them dig holes in the ground.

They use the holes for shelter.

Write two things that help prairie dogs live in their environment.

_____

_____

Circle the part of the prairie dog that helps it dig holes for shelter.

89

Desert Environment

A desert is a land environment.
A **desert** is land that is very dry.
A desert gets very little rain or snow.
Some deserts are very cold.
Plants grow in deserts.
Plants in deserts hold water.
Many animals get the water they need from the plants they eat.

Underline words that tell about deserts.

Tell how getting water from food helps animals live in the desert.

Circle the part of the rabbit that helps keep it cool.

Write what helps the lizard live in the desert.

This desert is hot during the day. Light-colored skin helps this lizard keep cool.

Heat leaves the body of the rabbit through its big ears.

Waxy leaves help this plant hold water.

How do plants and animals live in water environments?

Envision It!

Draw an animal that might live in this environment.

Inquiry **Explore It!**

How do some turtles stay warm in winter?

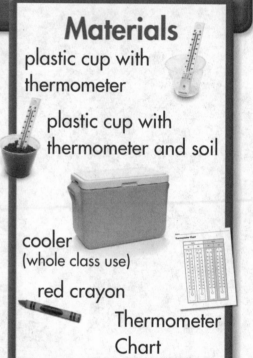

Materials

plastic cup with thermometer

plastic cup with thermometer and soil

cooler
(whole class use)

red crayon

Thermometer Chart

☐ **1. Record** the temperature in each cup. Use the Thermometer Chart.

☐ **2.** Put both cups in a cooler. **Predict.** Which cup will stay warmer?

_____

_____

☐ **3.** Wait 20 minutes. **Record** the temperature.

☐ **4.** Which stayed warmer? **(soil/air)**

Explain Your Results

5. Infer where turtles might live in the winter. Explain.

_____

_____

_____

UNLOCK THE BIG ?

I will know how some plants and animals can live in water environments.

Words to Know

wetland

ocean

Water Environments

Some animals live in water environments. They get what they need there.

Some plants live in water environments too. Some plants live on top of the water. Flat leaves help the plants float. Long roots soak up nutrients in the water. Some plants live underwater.

Underline sentences that tell about plants that float on top of the water.

Newts are a kind of animal. They live part of their lives in water. They find food and shelter there.

93

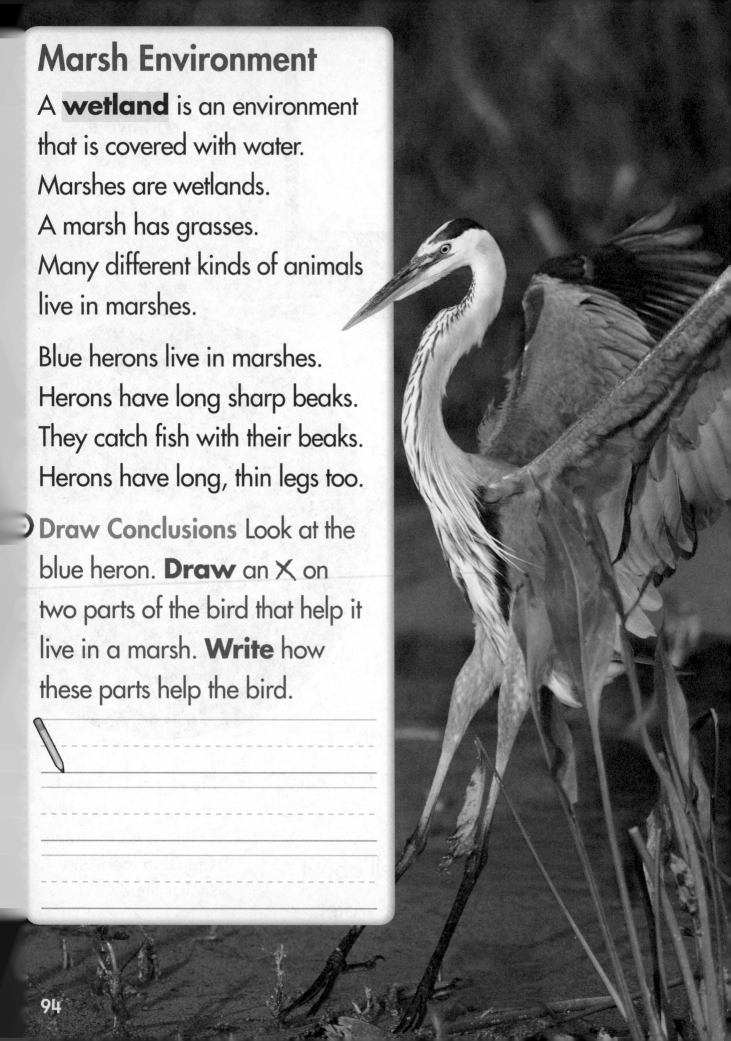

Marsh Environment

A **wetland** is an environment that is covered with water. Marshes are wetlands. A marsh has grasses. Many different kinds of animals live in marshes.

Blue herons live in marshes. Herons have long sharp beaks. They catch fish with their beaks. Herons have long, thin legs too.

Draw Conclusions Look at the blue heron. **Draw** an X on two parts of the bird that help it live in a marsh. **Write** how these parts help the bird.

Swamp Environment

Swamps are wetlands.

A swamp has soft, wet land.

A swamp has many trees.

Alligators live in some swamps.

Alligators are good swimmers.

Alligators use their long,
strong tails to help them swim.

Go Green

Wetlands
Find out about
wetlands in your state.
Write what plants and
animals live there.
How does your state
help protect wetlands?

Write why being a good swimmer
would help an alligator live in a swamp.

Draw an ✗ on the
part of the alligator
that helps it swim.

Ocean Environment

An **ocean** is a large body of salty water.

Some parts of the ocean are deep.

Fish live in the ocean.
Fish have gills.
Gills let fish take in oxygen from the water.
Fish have fins.
Fins help fish swim.

Plants need sunlight to make food.
Ocean plants live where there is light.
The deep ocean is dark.
Plants do not live there.

Underline the sentence that tells how gills help fish live in the ocean.

Write why plants do not live in the deep ocean.

Draw an X on the parts of the fish that help it swim.

gills

fins

What plants and animals no longer live on Earth?

Circle the animals that you think no longer live on Earth.

my planet diary   Did You Know?

Read Together

Many different plants lived on Earth long ago. These plants did not have flowers. Some of these plants had seeds.

One kind of plant that lived long ago is the seed fern. Seed ferns grew seeds. These seed ferns looked like small trees. They had leaves like the ferns that we see today.

Write about a plant in the picture.

_____

_____

UNLOCK THE BIG ? I will know some plants and animals that no longer live on Earth.

Words to Know

extinct   fossil

Extinct Plants and Animals

Some plants and animals are extinct. **Extinct** means they no longer live on Earth.

Some plants and animals became extinct very long ago.

Other plants and animals became extinct not so long ago.

Underline what extinct means.

◉ **Compare and Contrast Write** how a pterosaur and a bird are alike.

_____

- - - - - - - - - - -

_____

- - - - - - - - - - -

_____

The dusky seaside sparrow is extinct. The last one died in 1987.

pterosaur

99

Fossils

Fossils help us learn about extinct plants and animals.
A **fossil** is a print or part of a plant or animal that lived long ago.
A fossil can show the shape of a plant or animal.
A fossil can show the size of a plant or animal.

plant fossil

Look at the picture.
Tell about the fossil.

Write how we know animals lived on Earth long ago.

_____

_____

_____

_____

Lightning Lab

Extinct Animals

Learn about an animal that is extinct. Share what you learn with your class.

Dinosaurs

Dinosaurs are extinct animals.

You can learn about dinosaurs.

You can study dinosaur fossils.

Look at the dinosaur fossil below.

Draw what you think this dinosaur looked like.

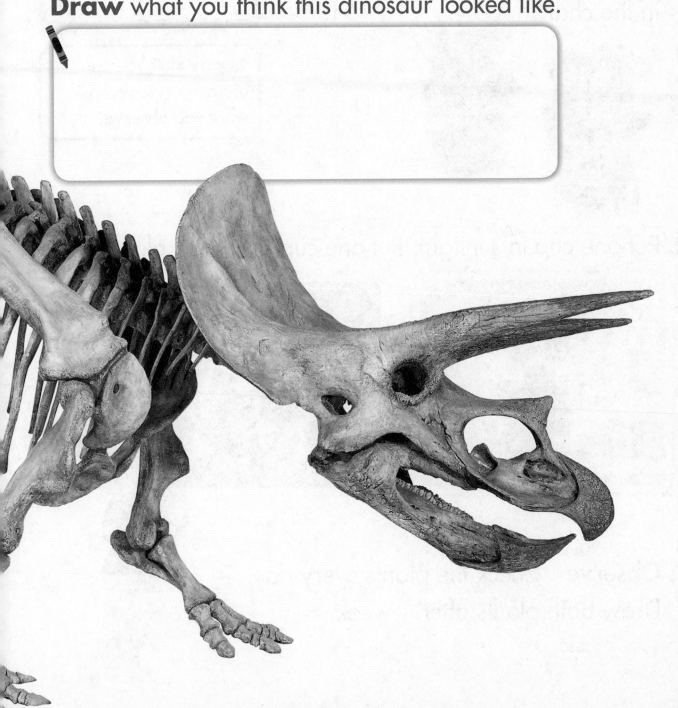

Do plants need light?

Materials

2 cups
with grass

water

Follow a Procedure

☑ **1.** Water both plants.
Draw both plants
in the chart.

Inquiry Skill You can
use a chart to record
what you **observe.**

☑ **2.** Put one cup in sunlight. Put one cup in a dark place.

☑ **3. Observe** Check the plants every day.
Draw both plants after 1 week.

Observations

Sunlight	Dark
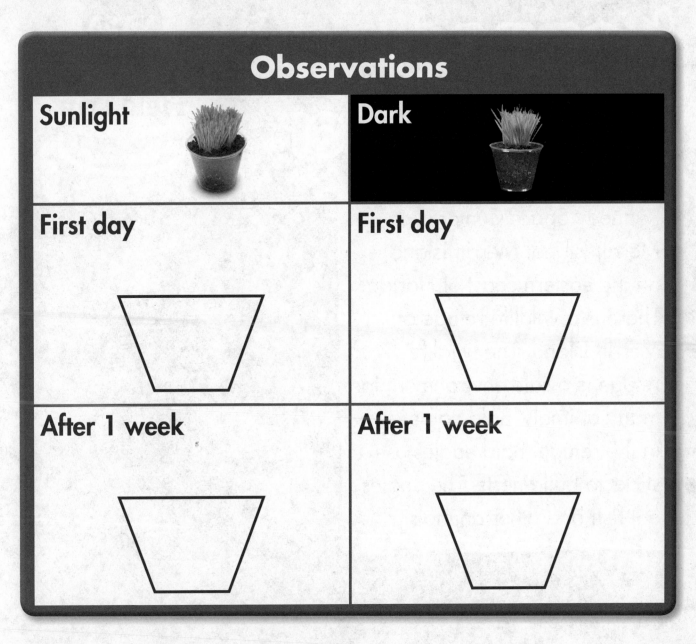	
First day	First day
After 1 week	After 1 week

Analyze and Conclude

4. Which plant grew better?

5.  **Infer** Look at your **observations.**
   Do plants need light? Explain.

Kennedy Space Center

Kennedy Space Center is on Merritt Island. Merritt Island is on the eastern coast of Florida. There is a wildlife refuge on Merritt Island. The wildlife refuge is a safe environment for many animals. Bald eagles live in the refuge. Bald eagles use sticks to build nests. The eagles eat fish and other animals.

Write two things a bald eagle needs.

Vocabulary Smart Cards

nonliving
living
need
nutrients
shelter
environment
forest
prairie
desert
wetland
ocean
extinct
fossil

Play a Game!

Cut out the cards. Put one set of cards word side up. Put another set of cards word side down. Match the word with the definition.

nutrients

nutrientes

nonliving

sin vida

shelter

albergue

living

vivo

environment

medio ambiente

need

necesidad

things that do not grow and change on their own

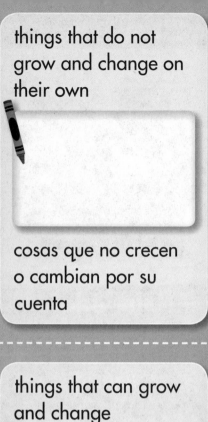

cosas que no crecen o cambian por su cuenta

materials that living things need

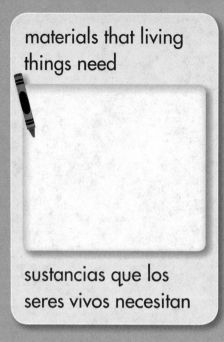

sustancias que los seres vivos necesitan

things that can grow and change

seres que pueden crecer y cambiar

a safe place

lugar seguro

something a living thing must have to live

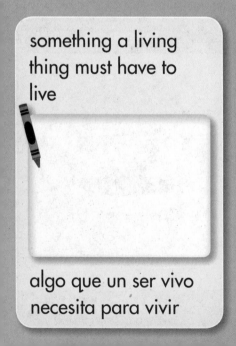

algo que un ser vivo necesita para vivir

all living and nonliving things in one place

todos los seres vivos y sin vida que hay en un lugar

fossil

fósil

wetland

pantanal

forest

bosque

ocean

océano

prairie

pradera

extinct

extinto

desert

desierto

environment that has many trees and other plants

medio ambiente que tiene muchos árboles y otras plantas

environment that is covered with water

medio ambiente cubierto de agua

a print or part of a plant or animal that lived long ago

huella o parte de una planta o animal que vivió hace mucho tiempo

environment that is covered with grasses

medio ambiente cubierto de pasto

environment that is a large body of salty water

medio ambiente que es un gran cuerpo de agua salada

environment that is very dry

medio ambiente que es muy seco

no longer live on Earth

no vive más en la Tierra

Lesson 1

What are nonliving and living things?

- Nonliving things do not grow or change.
- Living things can grow and change.

Lesson 2

What do living things need?

- Plants need air, water, light, and nutrients.
- Animals need air, water, food, and shelter.

Lesson 3

How do plants and animals live in land environments?

- Forests, prairies, and deserts are land environments.

Lesson 4

How do plants and animals live in water environments?

- Wetlands and oceans are water environments.
- Gills help fish live in water environments.

Lesson 5

What plants and animals no longer live on Earth?

- You can learn about extinct plants and animals from fossils.

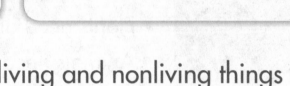
Lesson 1

1. Vocabulary Draw two nonliving things.

2. Contrast Write one way living and nonliving things are different.

_____

- -

_____

Lesson 2

◉ **3. Draw Conclusions** What does the baby fox use for shelter?

_____

- -

_____

Lesson 3

4. What helps bears live in forests?
Fill in the bubble.

Ⓐ gills   Ⓒ big ears

Ⓑ sharp claws   Ⓓ light-colored skin

Lesson 4

5. Vocabulary (Circle) the two wetland environments.

Lesson 5

6. **Explain** How can people learn about plants and animals that lived long ago?

_____

_____

Got it?

☐ **Stop!** I need help with _____

_____

_____

▶ **Go!** Now I know _____

_____

_____

How is a young orangutan like its mother?

Plants and Animals

Try It! How are flowers alike and different?

Lesson 1 What are some groups of living things?

Lesson 2 What are some parts of plants?

Lesson 3 How do plants grow?

Lesson 4 How do some animals grow?

Lesson 5 How are living things like their parents?

Lesson 6 How are groups of living things different?

Investigate It! How do different seeds grow?

Tell one way the baby and its mother are alike.

THE BIG ? **How are living things alike and different?**

Go to www.myscienceonline.com and click on:

Untamed Science
Ecogeeks answer your questions.

Got it? 60-Second Video
Lesson reviewed in a minute!

How are flowers alike and different?

☐ **1.** Take a flower apart.

☐ **2. Classify** Group the parts that are alike.

Materials

hand lens

paper

different flowers

Inquiry Skill
Classify means to sort things into groups that are alike and different.

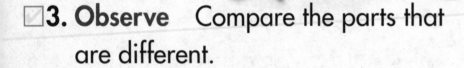

☐ **3. Observe** Compare the parts that are different.

Explain Your Results

4. Communicate How are the parts alike?

_____

5. How are the parts different?

_____

_____

_____

⊙ Compare and Contrast

You **compare** when you tell how things are alike.

You **contrast** when you tell how things are different.

grizzly bear

Two Kinds of Bears

Grizzly bears live in North America.

Pandas live in Asia.

Both bears have fur.

One bear has brown fur.

The other bear has black and white fur.

panda

Practice It!

Write how the grizzly bear and panda are alike and different.

Compare	Contrast

What are some groups of living things?

Envision It!

Tell one way you can group the animals in the pictures.

MY PLANET DIARY

Did You Know?

Read Together

What do you think this picture shows?

It lives underwater. It is a group of animals. It can be many different, beautiful colors. Groups of this make up reefs near coastlines.

Do you know what it is yet? It is coral.

The coral in the picture is called brain coral.

Why do you think it has that name?

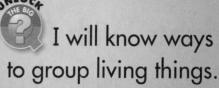
Word to Know

backbone

Groups of Living Things

Plants and animals are living things.
You can group living things in
different ways.
You can group living things by size.
You can group living things by color.
You can group living things by shape.
Scientists group living things too.

cardinal

⊙ **Compare and Contrast Write** how
the cardinal and the betta fish are
alike and different.

betta

Compare	Contrast

117

Plants With Flowers

There are two main plant groups.
One group of plants grows flowers.
The other group of plants does not grow flowers.

Plants with flowers make seeds.
Seeds grow in the flowers.
Plants with flowers grow in many places.

Draw a plant that grows flowers.

At-Home Lab

Plant Groups
Collect pictures of plants.
Work with an adult.
Group the pictures.
One group should be plants that grow flowers.
The other group should be plants that do not grow flowers.

Flowers grow on some trees.

Plants Without Flowers

Some plants do not have flowers.

Some plants have cones.

Seeds grow inside the cones.

Some plants do not have flowers
or cones.

These plants do not make any seeds.

These plants often grow in wet places.

(Circle) the plants that make seeds.

Name two plants that do not
grow flowers.

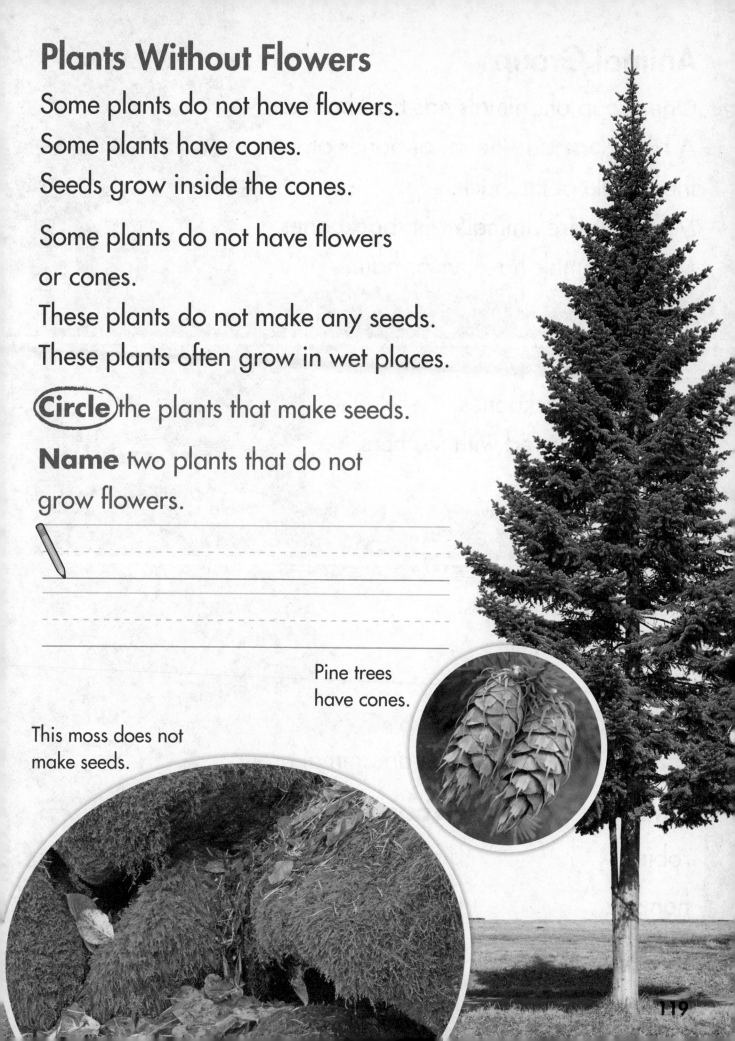

Pine trees
have cones.

This moss does not
make seeds.

119

Animal Groups

One group of animals has backbones. A **backbone** is the set of bones along the middle of the back. Mammals are animals with backbones. Most mammals have fur or hair.

moose

Birds have backbones.
Birds are covered with feathers.
Birds have wings.

oriole

Fish have backbones.
Fish live in water.
Fish have scales.

rockfish

Match each animal with an animal group.

Animal	Group
robin	bird
hamster	fish
goldfish	mammal

Reptiles have backbones.
Most reptiles have dry skin.
Reptiles have scales.

turtle

Amphibians have backbones. Amphibians have smooth, wet skin.

salamander

Another group of animals does not have backbones.
This is the largest group of animals.
Insects are part of this group.
All insects have six legs.

ant

Circle the insect.

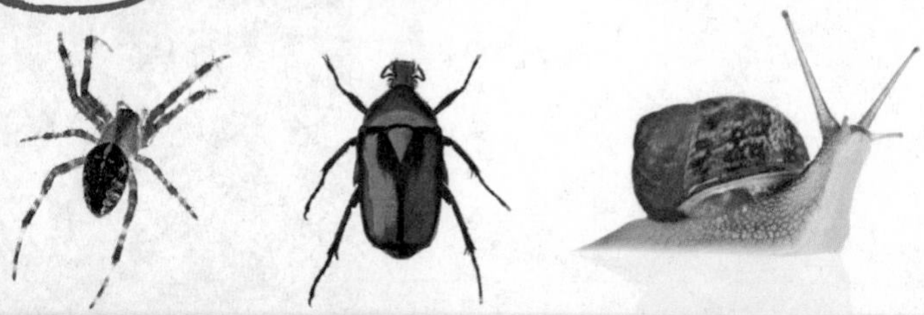

121

What are some parts of plants?

Envision It!

Tell what plant parts you see.

MY PLANET DiARY

Did You Know?

Read Together

Most of the ground in the tundra is frozen. Do you think plants will grow in the tundra?

_____

Only a few inches of soil in the tundra are not frozen. Plant roots need space to grow underground. Some plants without roots can grow in the tundra. Mosses are plants. Mosses do not have roots. Mosses can grow in the tundra.

Do you think trees with long roots grow in the tundra? Explain.

_____

_____

Draw the missing tulip parts.

Words to Know

root   stem
leaf

Parts of Plants

Plants have different parts.
The parts help the plant live and grow.
The parts help the plant get what it needs.

An iris and a tulip are plants.
They have the same parts.
They do not look alike.

iris

⊙ **Compare and Contrast** **Write** how the iris and the tulip are alike and different.

Compare

Contrast

123

Roots, Stems, and Leaves

Many plants have roots.
Roots hold the plant in the ground.
Roots take in water.

Many plants have leaves and stems too.
The **stem** takes water from the roots
to other parts of the plant.
The **leaf** makes food for the plant.

Draw an arrow to show how
water will move inside the plant.

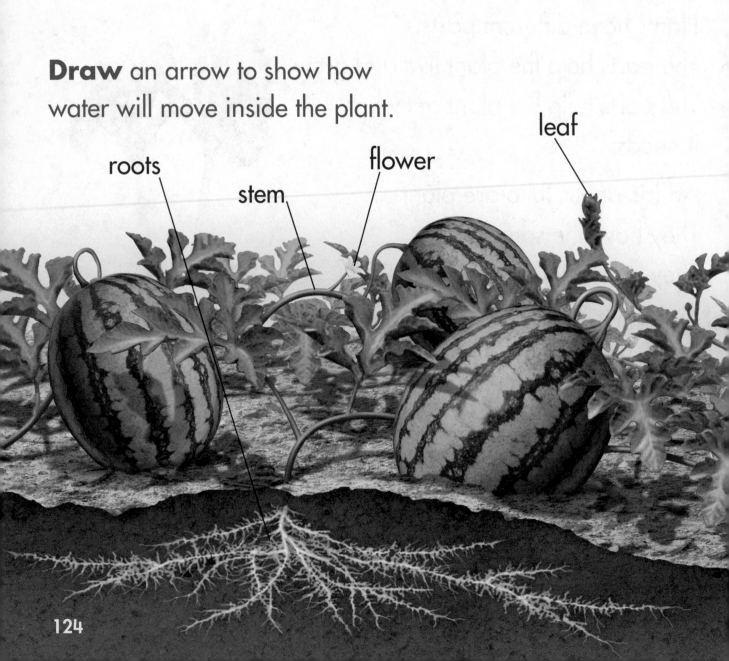

roots

stem

flower

leaf

Flowers and Fruit

Many plants have flowers.
Seeds come from flowers.
Fruits come from flowers too.
Fruits have seeds.

Circle the part of the rose
plant where seeds come from.

Draw a line from the word to
the plant part on the rose.

roots   stem   flowers   leaves

Lightning Lab

Grow a Plant
Get a cup of dirt.
Put a few seeds in
it. Put the cup in a
warm and sunny
area. Water the seeds
every day. Tell others
what parts of your
plant are growing.

How do plants grow?

Tell what you know about seeds and plants.

Inquiry Explore It!

How does a seed grow?

☑ **1.** Put the seeds and towel in a bag. Seal. Put in a warm place.

☑ **2. Observe** every other day. **Record**.

Materials

6 pinto bean seeds on a wet paper towel

resealable plastic bag

hand lens

Day 1	
Day 3	
Day 5	
Day 7	

Explain Your Results

3. Predict what will happen next.

_____

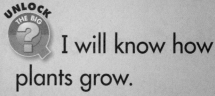
Words to Know
....
life cycle
seedling

Seeds to Trees

The way a living thing grows and changes is called a **life cycle.**

An oak seed is called an acorn.
Plant an acorn in the ground.
An oak seedling grows.
A **seedling** is a very young plant.

An oak seedling has a thin stem.
An oak seedling has small leaves.
The seedling grows into a tall tree.

Draw a line from the label to the picture.

(grown oak tree)

(oak seedling)

(oak seed)

127

Life Cycle of a Plant

A seedling grows from the seed.

Roots grow downward.

A stem grows upward.

The plant grows into an adult plant.

Some plants make flowers.

The flowers make seeds.

The seeds may grow into a new plant.

The life cycle starts again.

Tell how the pepper plant grows.

⊙ **Draw Conclusions**

What might happen if a seed did not get water?

The life cycle starts with a pepper seed.

Inside the peppers are the plant's seeds. The seeds may grow into new plants.

128

A seedling grows. It has roots and a stem.

Go Green

Helpful Houseplants
Plants need air to make food. Some plants clean the air as they make food. Discuss why this is good for people and pets.

The seedling grows into an adult plant. The plant grows flowers.

The flowers grow peppers.

How do some animals grow?

SC.1.L.17.1

Draw how the pig will look when it is grown.

MY PLANET DiARY

Fact or Fiction?

Read Together

All eggs from birds are the same, right? No, eggs can be very different. Think about eggs you get from the store. They are mostly the same size and color. These eggs come from chickens. Ostrich eggs are as big as a grapefruit. They are the biggest eggs in the world. Robin eggs are often blue. Quail eggs can be speckled.

Tell how the ostrich egg and the robin egg are alike and different.

quail egg

robin egg

ostrich egg

Word to Know

nymph

Animal Life Cycles

Animals have life cycles.
A life cycle is the way a living
thing grows and changes.

A goat is an animal.
A baby goat looks like its parents.
The baby goat grows and changes.
A grown goat may have young
of its own.
The life cycle begins again.

Number the goats in the order
of their life cycle.

Life Cycle of a Sea Turtle

A sea turtle is an animal.

A sea turtle starts life as an egg.

Soon the baby sea turtle is ready to hatch.

Baby sea turtles have an egg tooth. The egg tooth helps them break open the eggshell.

A baby sea turtle comes out of the egg.

Underline how a turtle uses its egg tooth.

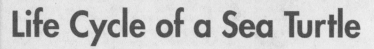

sea turtle eggs

grown sea turtle

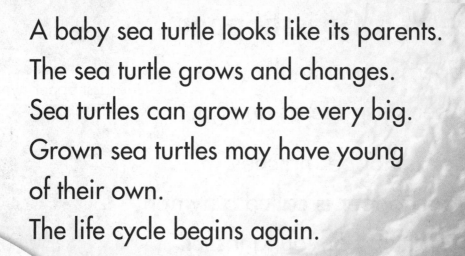

A baby sea turtle looks like its parents.
The sea turtle grows and changes.
Sea turtles can grow to be very big.
Grown sea turtles may have young
of their own.
The life cycle begins again.

baby sea turtle

young sea turtle

Draw arrows to show the
life cycle of the sea turtle.

Life Cycle of a Grasshopper

A grasshopper is an animal.

A grasshopper starts life as an egg.

The young grasshopper hatches.

A young grasshopper is called a nymph.

A **nymph** is a kind of young insect.

Nymphs look like their parents.

Nymphs do not have wings.

grasshopper nymph

grasshopper eggs

Circle the dragonfly nymph. **Tell** how you know it is a nymph.

A grown grasshopper has wings.
Grown grasshoppers may have
young of their own.
The life cycle begins again.

At-Home Lab

Life Cycle
Learn about the life
cycle of an animal.
Make a poster of the
animal's life cycle.

◉ **Compare and Contrast**
Write how a grown grasshopper
is different from a nymph.

grown grasshopper

How are living things like their parents?

Tell how the animals are alike and different.

 **Inquiry** **Explore It!**

How are babies and parents alike and different?

☐ **1.** Look at the pictures.
Talk about what you **observe.**

☐ **2. Classify** Play baby bingo.
Match the parent with its baby.

Explain Your Results

3. Communicate Which babies look like their parents?

_____

_____

List the babies that do not look like their parents.

_____

_____

Materials

baby bingo card

bingo chips

Baby Bingo Card

UNLOCK
THE BIG
?

I will know that plants and animals look like their parents.

Word to Know

parent

Plants and Their Parents

A **parent** is a living thing
that has young.
Plants and their parents are alike.
Plants and their parents can have
the same leaf shape.

Plants and their parents are
different too.
Plants and their parents
can have different
colored flowers.

Draw a line from
the young plant to
its parent.

young plant

137

How Animals and Their Parents Are Alike

Young animals are like their parents.
Many animals look like their parents.
Many animals have the same shape
as their parents.
Animals and their parents can have
the same number of legs.

<u>Underline</u> one way young animals
and their parents can be alike.

Draw what the lizard's parent
might look like.

The dog and its parent
have the same shape.

How Animals and Their Parents Are Different

Young animals and their parents are different too.

Young animals and their parents can be different colors.

Young animals are smaller than their parents.

◎ **Compare and Contrast**

Write how the young chickens are different from their parent.

_____

The cat and its kitten are different colors.

Lesson 6

How are groups of living things different?

Envision It!

Color the daisy.

Inquiry **Explore It!**

How are bodies different?

 1. Have a partner trace your left foot. Use the Footprint Sheet.

2. Put your footprint on the wall. Your teacher will tell you where.

3. Observe all the feet.

Explain Your Results

4. Draw a Conclusion

How are the feet alike and different?

Materials

tape (whole class use)

Footprint Sheet

UNLOCK THE BIG ？ I will know how groups of living things are alike and different.

Word to Know

herd

Kinds of Plants

Plants live all around the world.
Plants of one kind are alike.
Petunias are a kind of plant.
Petunias all have fuzzy, green leaves.
Plants of one kind are different too.
Look at the pictures.
One petunia plant has pink flowers.
The other petunia plant has purple flowers.

◉ **Compare and Contrast**

Tell how petunias are alike.
Write how these petunias are different.

141

Kinds of Animals

Animals of one kind are alike.

Giraffes are a kind of animal.

The picture shows a herd of giraffes.

A **herd** is a group of animals of one kind
that stays together.

Giraffes have four legs and two eyes.

Giraffes have spots too.

Underline one way giraffes are alike.

Draw another giraffe in the herd.

Different Animals of One Kind

Animals of one kind are different too.

Some giraffes have darker spots than others.

Some giraffes have longer necks than others.

Giraffes with longer necks can reach
leaves on tall trees.

Short giraffes cannot reach as high.

Fill in the words **long**, **spots**, and **short**.

Across

1. ____ giraffes cannot reach as high.

Down

2. ___ necks help giraffes reach leaves.

3. _____ on some giraffes are darker.

Lightning Lab

Alike and Different
Find two of the same kind of plant or animal. Tell how they are alike. Tell how they are different.

143

How do different seeds grow?

Follow a Procedure

☑ **1.** Fold a paper towel. Put it inside a cup.

☑ **2.** Ball up another paper towel. Put it inside the same cup.

☑ **3.** Wet the paper towels with water.

☑ **4.** Put the bean seeds in the cup.

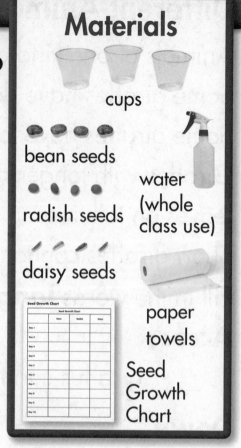

Materials

cups

bean seeds

radish seeds

daisy seeds

water (whole class use)

paper towels

Seed Growth Chart

Inquiry Skill

You use a chart to help **collect data**.

Be careful! Wash your hands when you finish.

☐ **5. Repeat** the steps with radish seeds.
Repeat the steps with daisy seeds.

☐ **6. Observe** the seeds for 10 days.
Collect Data Draw what you see.
Use the Seed Growth Chart.

Analyze and Conclude

7. How did the different seeds grow the same?
How did the seeds grow different?

_____

_____

_____

_____

8. UNLOCK THE BIG ? **Infer** If you planted radish seeds and bean seeds in your garden, which would grow first?

_____

_____

_____

_____

_____

_____

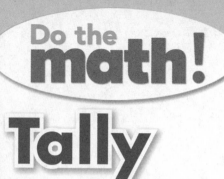

Do the math!

Tally

You can use tally marks to record information.

This is a tally mark. |

These are 5 tally marks. ||||

This chart shows how many trees are in the picture.

Living Things	Tally	Total
Tree			1
Bird		
Lizard		

Write tally marks to record how many birds and lizards are in the picture. Then write the totals.

Find one more living thing in the picture. **Record** the information in the chart.

146

Vocabulary Smart Cards

backbone
root
stem
leaf
life cycle
seedling
nymph
parent
herd

Play a Game!

Cut out the cards.

Work with a partner. Put the cards word side up.

Have your partner put the cards word side down.

Work together to match the word with the definition.

147

leaf

hoja

backbone

columna vertebral

life cycle

ciclo de vida

root

raíz

seedling

plántula

stem

tallo

the set of bones along the middle of the back

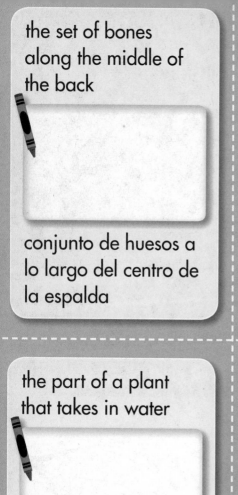

conjunto de huesos a lo largo del centro de la espalda

the part of a plant that makes food

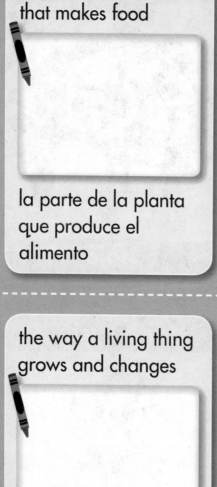

la parte de la planta que produce el alimento

the part of a plant that takes in water

la parte de la planta que toma el agua

the way a living thing grows and changes

manera en que un ser vivo crece y cambia

the part of a plant that takes water from the roots to the leaves

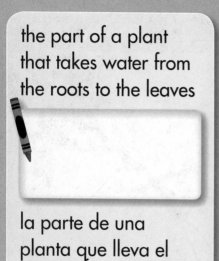

la parte de una planta que lleva el agua de las raíces a las hojas

a very young plant

planta muy joven

nymph

ninfa

parent

progenitor

herd

manada

a kind of young insect

tipo de insecto joven

a living thing that has young

ser vivo que tiene crías

a group of animals of one kind that stay together

grupo de animales del mismo tipo que están juntos

REVIEW THE BIG **?** How are living things alike and different?

Lesson 1

What are some groups of living things?

- One group of plants has flowers.
- One group of animals has backbones.

Lesson 2

What are some parts of plants?

- Roots and stems help plants get water.
- Leaves make food for the plant.

Lesson 3

How do plants grow?

- Plants change during their life cycle.
- A seedling is a very young plant.

Lesson 4

How do some animals grow?

- Animals change during their life cycle.
- A young grasshopper is called a nymph.

Lesson 5

How are living things like their parents?

- Parents and young can be the same shape.
- Parents and young can be different colors.

Lesson 6

How are groups of living things different?

- One kind of flower can be different colors.
- Animals in a herd are alike and different.

Chapter Review

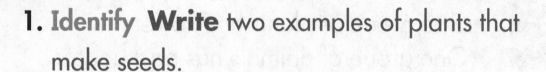 How are living things alike and different?

Lesson 1

1. **Identify Write** two examples of plants that make seeds.

_____

2. Which group of animals has fur or hair?
Fill in the bubble.

- Ⓐ mammals
- Ⓑ birds
- Ⓒ reptiles
- Ⓓ insects

Lesson 2

3. **Vocabulary Label** the parts of the plant.

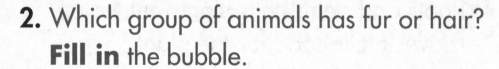

Lesson 3

4. **Vocabulary Write** about how a seedling changes.

_____

_____

Lesson 4

5. Apply Draw a
grown grasshopper.

Lesson 5

6. Compare and Contrast How is a young dog different
from its parents?

_____

Lesson 6

7. Describe How does a longer neck help a giraffe?

_____

_____

_____

Got it?

☐ **Stop!** I need help with _____

_____

▶ **Go!** Now I know _____

How can a mouse's color help keep it safe from hawks?

Materials

white beans

black beans

white beans with black spots

paper plate

clock with second hand (or timer or stopwatch)

Inquiry Skill
You plan an **experiment** when you design a way to answer a scientific question.

Ask a question.

white beans = field where mice live
white beans with spots = light mice
black beans = dark mice

How can a mouse's color help keep it safe from hunting hawks?

Make a prediction.

1. Will light-colored mice or dark-colored mice be easier to see in a field?

   (a) light-colored mice

   (b) dark-colored mice

Plan a fair test.

Use the same number of white beans with spots and black beans.

Design your test.

☑ **2.** List your steps.

Do your test.

☑ **3.** Follow your steps.

Collect and record data.

☑ **4.** Fill in the chart.

Tell your conclusion.

5. Which mice in your model were harder to see?

6. Infer Which mice are harder to see in a light habitat?

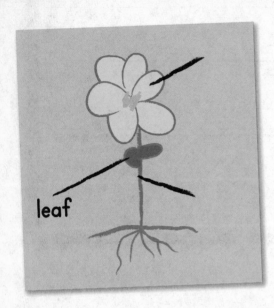

leaf

Draw a Picture

- Draw a picture of a plant.
- Show and label the parts of the plant.
- Tell how the parts help the plant.

Grow Plants

- Gather soil and sand.
- Find out if plants grow better in soil or in sand.

Write a Poem

- Choose an animal.
- Write a poem about what the animal needs.
- Draw a picture to go with your poem.

Using Scientific Methods

1. Ask a question.
2. Make a hypothesis.
3. Plan a fair test.
4. Do your test.
5. Collect and record data.
6. Tell your conclusion.

Earth Science

What does the rock look like?

Earth and Sky

Tell about the land in the picture.

 What can you tell about Earth and sky?

Go to www.myscienceonline.com and click on: ⊗

 Untamed Science
Watch the Ecogeeks in this wild video.

Got it? **60-Second Video**
Take one minute to learn science!

Explore It! Animation
Watch your experiment online!

How much water and land are on Earth?

☑ 1. **Observe** Find water and land on the globe.

☑ 2. Toss the globe.

☑ 3. Catch the globe.

☑ 4. **Collect Data** Is the tip of your finger on water or land? Put a mark in the chart.

Materials
inflatable globe

Inquiry Skill
You **interpret data** when you use your chart to answer a question.

Water	Land

☑ 5. Repeat the steps 9 more times.

Explain Your Results

6. **Interpret Data** Use your chart to answer the question. Is there more water or land on Earth? Explain.

_____

_____

_____

⊙ Compare and Contrast

You **compare** when you tell
how things are alike.
You **contrast** when you tell
how things are different.

Appalachian Mountains

Mountains

Mountains are very high.
The Rocky Mountains are rough.
The Appalachian Mountains
are not.
The Rocky Mountains are higher
than the Appalachian Mountains.

Rocky Mountains

Practice It!

Write how the mountains are alike and different.

Compare	Contrast

161

my planet diary

Connections

Long ago people known as the Incas lived in the mountains in South America. It was hard to grow crops in the mountains. The Incas built flat pieces of land called terraces so they could grow crops. Today some people do not have land to grow crops and other plants. They use pots and planters.

Write how you might grow plants where you live.

_____

_____

_____

UNLOCK
THE BIG
?

I will know that land, water, and living things are found on Earth.

Word to Know

soil

Land, Water, and Air

Earth is made of many things.

Earth has land.

Earth has water.

The surface of Earth has more water than land.

Earth has air all around it.

Color the land green.
Color the water blue.

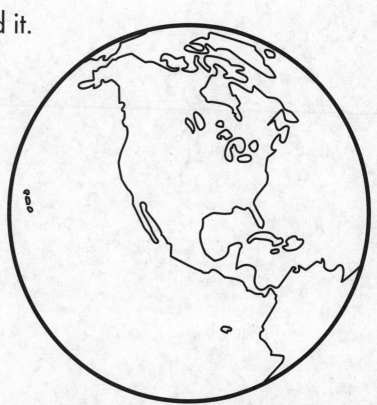

Kinds of Land

Earth has many different kinds of land.
Plains are large, flat areas of land.
Hills are where the land gets higher.
Mountains are the highest kind of land.
An island is land with water all
around it.

Label the plains,
mountains, and island.

The Blue Ridge Mountains
rise above the land
around them.

Rocks and Soil

Earth's land has rocks and soil.

Rocks are hard.

Rocks can be many colors.

Soil is the top layer of Earth.

Soil can be soft.

<u>**Underline**</u> two things that are found on Earth.

rocks and soil

◉ **Compare and Contrast** **Write** one way rocks and soil are different.

At-Home Lab

Kinds of Landforms
Draw one kind of land near where you live. Draw another kind of land. Write how they are the same. Write how they are different.

Water on Earth

Earth has many places with water.

A river is water that flows across land.

Lakes have land all around them.

The ocean is a large area of salt water.

The ocean covers most of Earth.

Match the word to the picture.
Draw a line.

river   lake   ocean

Living Things

Living things are on land.
Living things are in soil.
Living things are in water.

Circle living things on land.
Draw an X on living things in water.

What are rocks and soil?

Tell how you can group the rocks.

Inquiry **Explore It!**

What are soils like?

☐ **1.** Put a spoonful of each soil on a paper plate.

☐ **2. Observe.** Draw. Show colors. Tell how each soil feels.

Materials

loam and sandy soil

paper plate   (whole class use)

hand lens   spoons

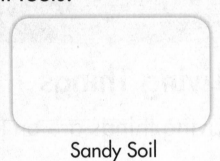

Loam   Sandy Soil

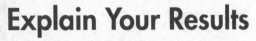

Be careful! Wash your hands when done.

Explain Your Results

3. Communicate   Describe what you see in the soil.

Word to Know

humus

Rocks

Rocks are nonliving things.
Rocks come from Earth.

Rocks can be different sizes.
Rocks can be different shapes.
Rocks can be different colors.
Rocks can feel smooth or rough.

Write about the rock in the
picture.

_____

_____

_____

_____

Crystals formed inside this rock.

169

Parts of Soil

Tiny bits of rock are in soil.
These tiny bits of rock are
different sizes.
Bits of clay are the smallest size.
Bits of silt are bigger than bits of clay.
Bits of sand are the biggest size.

Humus is in soil.
Humus is small pieces of dead
plants and animals.
Air and water are in soil too.

Underline the parts of soil that are
made from rock.

Circle the soil part made of small
pieces of dead plants and animals.

clay

soil with silt

sand

humus

170

Clay Soil

Soils from different places
can have different parts.
Soils can be different colors.
Soils can be smooth or rough.

Clay soil is made mostly of clay.
Clay soil can feel smooth and sticky.
Some clay soil is red.
Clay soil does not have a lot of air.
Many plants do not grow well in clay soil.

Write about the soil in the picture.

At-Home Lab

Describe Soil
Work with an adult.
Look at some soil.
What color is it? How
does it feel? What
parts do you see?

This soil is
made of clay.

171

Soil With Silt and Sandy Soil

Some soil is mostly made of silt.
Soil with silt can feel smooth.
Soil with silt is often brown.
Plants often grow well in soil
with silt.

Sandy soil is mostly made of sand.
Sandy soil feels dry and rough.
Often sandy soil is tan.
Sandy soil does not hold water well.
Most plants do not grow well
in sandy soil.

These hills have soil with silt.

⊙ **Compare and Contrast**

Write one way that soil with silt is different from sandy soil.

This desert has sandy soil.

loam

Loam

Loam has clay, silt, and sand.

Loam has humus too.

Loam feels wet.

Loam is often dark brown.

Loam has the right amount of water and air.

Plants grow well in loam soil.

Circle what is in loam.

Draw how you could use loam.

What changes land?

before

This volcano erupted.

Inquiry **Explore It!**

Materials

2 sandpaper blocks

How does Earth's surface move during an earthquake?

☑ **1.** Push the blocks together. Slide them past each other.

☑ **2.** Push the blocks together hard. Slide them past each other.

Explain Your Results

3. Did the blocks move smoothly both times? Explain.

4. Infer   An earthquake happens **(fast/slow)**. Tell why.

after

Tell how the land changed.

UNLOCK THE BIG ?

I will know some fast and slow ways Earth changes.

Words to Know

weathering
erosion

Changes on Earth

Earth is always changing.
Some changes happen fast.
A truck digs a hole in the ground.
This is a fast change.
Other changes are very slow.
A river flows through land.
This changes land slowly.

Underline a way Earth can change fast.

This truck moves rocks and soil.

The Colorado River makes the Grand Canyon wider and deeper.

Earthquakes and Volcanoes

Earthquakes happen fast.

An earthquake can cause land to crack.

Volcanoes cause fast changes too.

Volcanoes can explode.

Rock and ash from a volcano can cover land.

earthquake

volcano

⊙ **Compare and Contrast Write** how earthquakes and volcanoes are alike.

Weathering and Erosion

Weathering and erosion change land slowly.
Weathering is when water or ice breaks down rocks.
Erosion is when wind or water moves rocks and soil.
Weathering and erosion can take a long time!

weathering

erosion

Circle what causes weathering.
Underline what causes erosion.
Tell one change to land that happens fast and one that happens slowly.

Lightning Lab

Erosion
Pour sand into one end of a pan. Raise that end. Slowly pour water over the sand. Write where the sand goes.

How do people use natural resources?

Tell why you think people collect cans.

Inquiry **Explore It!**

How does a well work?

People need water. Some people get the water they need from wells.

☑ **1.** Put a tube in a bowl.
Pour gravel around the tube.
The tube is a **model** of a well.

☑ **2.** Make it rain. Pour water on the gravel.
Observe.

Explain Your Result

3. Infer How did the water move in your model?

_____

_____

_____

Materials

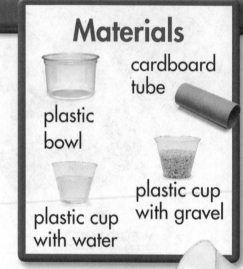

plastic bowl

cardboard tube

plastic cup with water

plastic cup with gravel

Words to Know

natural   reuse
resource   recycle
reduce

Natural Resources

People use Earth materials for
many things.

A **natural resource** is a useful
material found on Earth.

Water is a natural resource.

Rocks and soil are natural resources.

Plants and animals are natural
resources too.

Circle one natural resource in the picture.

Write how you use the natural resource.

Sunlight and Wood

Sunlight is a natural resource.

People use heat and light from the sun.

Sunlight makes plants grow.

Sunlight cannot be used up.

Wood is a natural resource.

People use wood to build many things.

People burn wood for heat.

People can plant trees to grow more wood.

Wood is used to build houses.

Circle the natural resource that cannot be used up.

Underline how people can get more wood.

Write about something else people make with wood.

_____

_____

_____

Oil and Copper

Oil is a natural resource.

Gasoline is made from oil.

People use energy from gasoline
to power cars.

Oil can be used up.

Copper is a natural resource.

People use copper to make wire.

Copper can be used up.

Suppose all the oil on Earth is used up.

Tell what you think might happen.

Gasoline is a source of energy.

Copper is a metal that comes
from Earth.

Reduce, Reuse, and Recycle

You can use natural resources wisely.
You can reduce what you use.
Reduce means to use less.
You can turn off the lights
when you leave a room.

You can reuse things.
Reuse means to use again.
You can wash glass jars
and use them again.

Tell one way you can reduce
how much paper you use.

Go Green

Care for Earth
Write a plan for how
you can care for
Earth. Share your plan
with your family. Do
your plan.

Draw one way you can
reuse a glass jar.

You can recycle.

Recycle means to make used materials into new things.

You can recycle paper, plastic, and glass. You can recycle many other things too.

Write one thing you use that is made from recycled material.

Milk jugs are used to make things like the bench below.

MADE OF RECYCLED MATERIALS

What is the sun?

Circle what the sun warms.

 Inquiry **Explore It!**

How can the sun make temperatures change?

☑ **1. Observe** the thermometers. Color in the lines on the chart.

☑ **2.** Put one in sunlight. Put one in shade.

☑ **3.** Wait. Observe. Color in the lines.

☑ **4.** Which thermometer warmed up more?

_____

_____

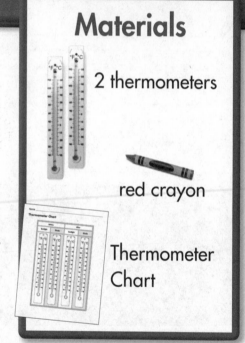

Materials

2 thermometers

red crayon

Thermometer Chart

Explain Your Results

5. Infer How did sunlight change the temperature?

_____

_____

UNLOCK
THE BIG
?

I will know ways
the sun helps and
harms things on Earth.

Word to Know

sun

The Nearest Star

A star is a big ball of hot gas.
The sun is a star.
The **sun** is the star that
is nearest to Earth.
The sun is bigger
than Earth.
The sun looks small
because it is far away.
You can see the sun
in the day sky.

The sun is very hot
and bright.

⊙ **Cause and Effect**
(Circle) the words that tell
why the sun looks small.

185

Why We Need the Sun

The sun helps us.

The sun warms the land.

The sun warms the water.

The sun warms the air.

Living things need heat from the sun.

The sun lights Earth.

Plants need light from the sun to grow.

We use light from the sun to see.

Write one reason why living things need the sun.

The sun makes the day sky bright.

Out in the Sun

The sun can harm us too.
It is important to be careful
in the sun.
Too much sun can hurt your
skin and eyes.
Sunscreen and a hat can
protect you from the sun.
Some sunglasses can protect
your eyes from the sun.
You should never look
at the sun.

Underline one way the
sun harms us.

Circle two things that
protect these children
from the sun.

Lightning Lab

Heat from the Sun
Get two pieces of
clay. Put one piece in
sunlight. Put the other
in shade. Wait 10
minutes. Write how
each feels.

What causes day and night?

Tell how day and night are different.

my planeT DiaRY   INVENTION!

Read Together

Scientists use telescopes to observe the night sky. The first telescope was invented by Hans Lippershey. Hans Lippershey invented the telescope over 400 years ago. Newer telescopes can help you see things in more detail. People have made many discoveries using telescopes.

Write what you would observe with a telescope.

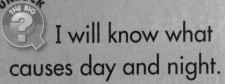

Word to Know

rotation

Day Sky

The sun is in the day sky.

The sun makes the day sky bright.

You may see clouds in the day sky.

You may see birds in the day sky.

Sometimes you can see the moon
in the day sky too.

day sky

Write about the day sky
in the picture.

189

Night Sky

The moon and stars are in the night sky.
You may see clouds in the night sky.
You may see birds in the night sky too.

night sky

Circle the things that can be in the night sky.

Moon

The moon moves around Earth.
Light from the sun shines on the moon.
You only see the part of the moon lit
by the sun.
The moon looks a little different
each night.
The moon looks the same again
about every 29 days.

Draw the different ways the
moon might look.

At-Home Lab

Changes in the Sky
Observe the sky when the sun rises. Observe the sky when the sun sets. Tell your family about what you see. Never look directly at the sun.

Sunrise and Sunset

The sun seems to rise each day. The sky becomes light. The sun seems to move across the sky during the day. The sun seems to set at night. The sky becomes dark.

Tell how the sky changes from day to night.

Day and Night

The sun looks like it is moving but it is not. Earth is moving. Earth spins around and around. One spin around is called a **rotation.** Earth makes one rotation every day.

Earth is always spinning.

It is day when your part of Earth faces toward the sun. It is night when your part of Earth faces away from the sun. The rotation of Earth causes day and night.

Write what causes day and night.

_____

_____

_____

_____

How can rocks crack?

Follow a Procedure

☐ **1.** Push the foil end of the sponge into the plaster. Keep the other end of the sponge out.

☐ **2.** Wait 1 day. Pull out the sponge. Do not pull out the foil. **Observe. Record.**

☐ **3.** Fill the foil with water. Put the cup in a freezer. Wait 1 day.

☐ **4.** Observe the cup. How has the plaster changed? Record your data.

Materials

plastic cup with plaster of paris

sponge with foil

water

safety goggles

latex-free gloves (optional)

Inquiry Skill

In an **investigation** you observe carefully and record your results.

Wear safety goggles.

Wash your hands if you get plaster on them.

Do not eat plaster or get it in your eyes.

Be careful!

Observations	
After 1 day	
After freezing	

Be careful! Wash your hands when you finish.

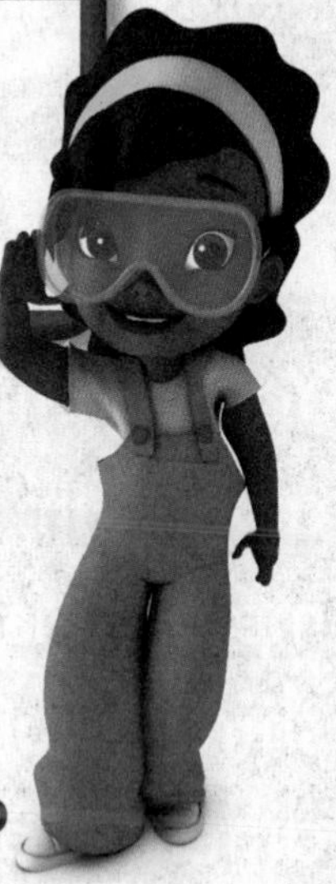

Analyze and Conclude

5. Draw a Conclusion What caused the changes?

6. Infer How are some cracks made in Earth's rocks?

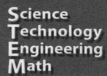

STEM

Read Together

Aluminum

You can find materials such as aluminum on Earth. Aluminum is a metal. It is not heavy. It is light. It is shiny. Aluminum is found in many different products. It is in foil and some cans. Aluminum is in some cars and trucks too. Engineers use aluminum to build parts of some cars and trucks. Cars and trucks made with aluminum are lighter than other cars and trucks. They use less gas. This helps the environment.

Melted aluminum is poured into molds and can become part of fire truck or an aluminum can.

Aluminum is a light metal. What other ways might engineers use aluminum?

_____

_____

_____

_____

Vocabulary Smart Cards

soil
humus
weathering
erosion
natural
 resource
reduce
reuse
recycle
sun
rotation

Play a Game!

Cut out the cards.

Work with a group.

Tape a card to the back of each group member.

Have each member guess what his or her word is by giving clues.

erosion

erosión

soil

suelo

natural resource

recurso natural

humus

humus

reduce

reducir

weathering

meteorización

the top layer of Earth

la capa superior de la Tierra

when wind or water moves rocks and soil

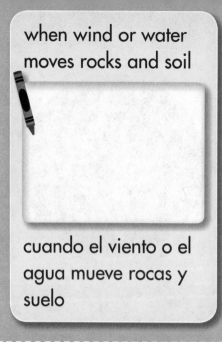

cuando el viento o el agua mueve rocas y suelo

small bits of dead plants and animals in soil

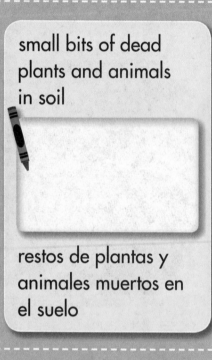

restos de plantas y animales muertos en el suelo

a useful material found in nature

material útil que se encuentra en la naturaleza

when water or ice breaks down rocks

cuando el agua o el hielo rompe las rocas

to use less

usar menos

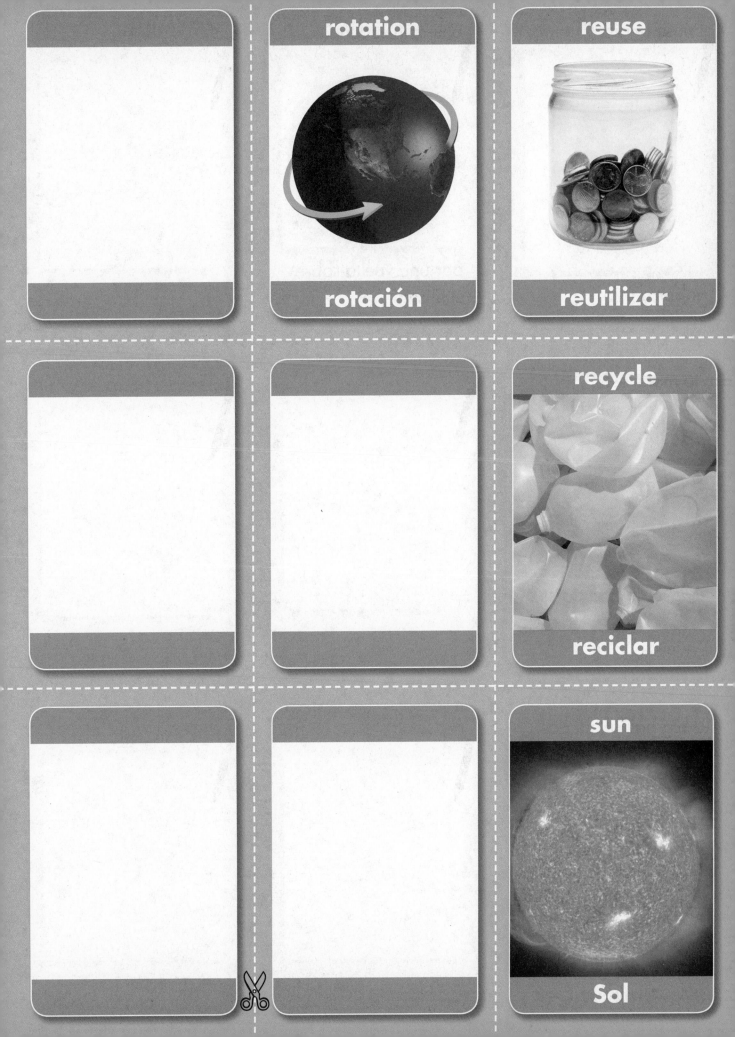

rotation

rotación

reuse

reutilizar

recycle

reciclar

sun

Sol

to use again

volver a usar

one spin around

dar una vuelta sobre
sí mismo

to make used
materials into new
materials

convertir materiales
usados en materiales
nuevos

a big ball of hot gas

bola muy grande de
gas caliente

Lesson 1

What is on Earth?

- Earth has different kinds of land and water.
- Rocks and soil are on Earth's surface.

Lesson 2

What are rocks and soil?

- Rocks can be different colors and shapes.
- Humus is in many kinds of soil.

Lesson 3

What changes land?

- Volcanoes and earthquakes change land.
- Weathering and erosion change land too.

Lesson 4

How do people use natural resources?

- Rocks and soil are natural resources.
- You can reduce, reuse, and recycle.

Lesson 5

What is the sun?

- The sun warms and lights Earth.
- The sun can harm your skin and eyes.

Lesson 6

What causes day and night?

- The sun makes the day sky bright.
- The rotation of Earth causes day and night.

Lesson 1

1. Exemplify Draw two things that are found on Earth.

Lesson 2

2. Apply Write about clay soil.

Lesson 3

◎ **3. Compare and Contrast Write** how erosion and earthquakes are different.

Lesson 4

4. Vocabulary Draw an ✗ on the natural resource.

Lesson 5

5. Explain Why do we need the sun?

Lesson 6

6. What is NOT seen in the night sky? **Fill in** the bubble.

Ⓐ birds   Ⓒ clouds

Ⓑ moon   Ⓓ sun

Got it?

☐ **Stop!** I need help with _____

▶ **Go!** Now I know _____

Where is the rain coming from?

Weather

 Try It! What is the weather like in different seasons?

Lesson 1 What is the water cycle?

Lesson 2 What is weather?

Lesson 3 How can you measure weather?

Lesson 4 What are the four seasons?

 Investigate It! How does water vapor condense?

Tell what you think the sky looks like when it is raining.

 How can you describe weather?

Go to www.myscienceonline.com and click on: ⊗

UntamedScience™
Watch the Ecogeeks in this wild video.

Got it? 60-Second Video
Review each lesson in 60 seconds!

my planet Diary
Fact or Fiction? Find out through Planet Diary.

I Will Know...
Interact with science to find out what you know.

What is the weather like in different seasons?

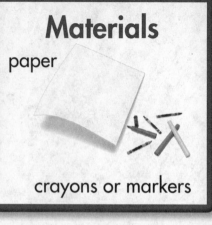

Materials

paper

crayons or markers

☐ **1. Observe** What season is it now?

_____

☐ **2.** What is the weather like today?

_____

_____

_____

Inquiry Skill

You can use what you learned to **predict**.

☐ **3.** Draw yourself outside in the season now.

☐ **4.** Draw yourself outside in the other seasons.

Explain Your Results

5. Predict what you will need to wear next season.

_____

_____

6. How does the weather change from season to season?

_____

_____

⊙ Sequence

To put things in **sequence** means to tell what happens first, next, and last.

Windy Weather

First, put a wind sock outside.

Next, check the wind sock.

Last, see the direction the wind blows.

Practice It!

Write the steps to follow.

First

| Put the wind sock outside. |

Next

Last

| See the direction the wind blows. |

What is the water cycle?

Draw a picture of where rain comes from.

Inquiry **Explore It!**

How can water change?

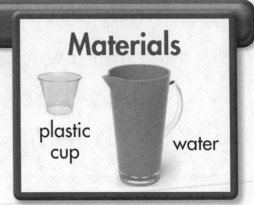

Materials

plastic cup

water

☐ **1.** Put water in a cup. Ask your teacher to mark the water line.

☐ **2.** Put the cup in a freezer. Wait 1 day.

☑ **3.** Compare the mark to the ice.

☑ **4.** Leave the cup out.

    Observe each day for 1 week. Discuss.

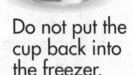

Do not put the cup back into the freezer.

Explain Your Results

5. Communicate What happens to the water over time?

_____

_____

_____

_____

Water Changes

Drip, drop, rain falls.
Puddles form on the ground.
The sun comes out.
Where does the water go?

Water in the puddles evaporates.
Evaporate means to change
from a liquid to a gas.

○ **Sequence** **Write** what happens last.

First

Puddles form.

Next

The sun comes out.

Last

209

The Water Cycle

Water moves into the air as a
gas when it evaporates.
Water that is a gas is called
water vapor.
You cannot see water vapor.
Water falls back to Earth from clouds.
This is called the water cycle.

Water evaporates from oceans.
Draw an X on another place where
water may evaporate.

Water vapor turns into drops
of water and ice as it cools.
This forms clouds.

Water evaporates and becomes
water vapor.

Look at the picture.
Follow the steps in the water cycle.

⊙ **Sequence** Water vapor turns into drops of water and ice as it cools. **Write** what happens next.

At-Home Lab

Evaporation
Place an ice cube in the sunlight. Wait. What happens to the ice cube? How long does it take? What happens next?

Water falls back to Earth as rain, snow, sleet, and hail.

Some water flows into rivers, lakes, and oceans.
The water cycle continues.

What is weather?

Envision It!

Tell what it is like in the picture.

my planet diary

Did You Know?

Read Together

Snowflakes might fall if the weather is very cold. Some snowflakes are tiny. Some snowflakes are very big. The largest snowflake ever recorded was found in Montana. The snowflake was about 15 inches across. It was also about 8 inches thick. That is a big snowflake!

Write what the air feels like when it is snowing.

_____

212

UNLOCK THE BIG ?

I will know how to describe weather. I will know how to stay safe in bad weather.

Word to Know

weather

Weather

Weather is what it is like outside.
Weather changes from day to day.
Weather may be windy or still.
Weather may be wet or dry.
Weather may be sunny or cloudy.
Different clouds bring different weather.

Dark clouds bring storms.

⦿ **Picture Clues** Look at the pictures.
Write how the clouds might look on a rainy day.

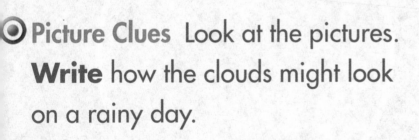

Fluffy white clouds are a sign of good weather.

213

Safety in Bad Weather

Storms can bring bad weather.
You can stay safe during storms.
A thunderstorm has rain,
lightning, and thunder.
You should find shelter
in a building or car.

thunderstorm

A tornado can happen
during a thunderstorm.
Tornadoes have very strong winds.
Go to a basement or a place
without windows.

Underline one way to stay safe
in a tornado.

Lightning Lab

Weather Safety
Put on a skit. Show
how to stay safe in
stormy weather.
Share your skit with
your class.

tornado

A hurricane is a very bad storm.
The wind blows very hard.
The rain is very heavy.
You can be safe in a hurricane.
You should stay inside and away from windows.

Tell what the weather is like in a hurricane.

hurricane

Snowstorms can bring lots of snow.
You should stay inside during a snowstorm.
You can prepare for a snowstorm.
You will need to have plenty of food and water.

Draw one thing you need during a snowstorm.

snowstorm

How can you measure weather?

Circle the tool that measures rain.

Inquiry Explore It!

When is it warm or cool?

Materials

thermometer

☑ **1.** Put the thermometer outside in the morning.

☑ **2.** What is the temperature? **Record.**

☑ **3.** What is the afternoon temperature?

Explain Your Results

4. When was it cooler? When was it warmer?

5. Infer Why did the temperature change?

UNLOCK
THE BIG
?
I will know how
to measure weather.

Word to Know

temperature

Measure Weather

People do different things
in different kinds of weather.
People may swim on a hot day.
People may ice skate on a cold day.

Some people measure the weather.
People use weather tools.
The tools help people know
what the weather is like.

⊙ **Picture Clues Write** one thing you
think the girl in the picture might do.

Weather Tools

A thermometer is a weather tool.

A thermometer measures temperature.

Temperature is how hot or cold
something is.

The numbers show the temperature.

The red line goes up as the air
gets warmer.

The red line goes down as the air
gets cooler.

(Circle) the thermometer that matches
the weather in the picture.

You can measure
temperature in
degrees Fahrenheit
and degrees Celsius.

More Weather Tools

A rain gauge measures rain.
The numbers tell how much rain
has fallen.

A wind vane shows wind direction.
Wind is moving air.
A wind vane points into the wind.

Look at the pictures.
Draw a line from each tool to
what it measures.
Tell a partner two things about
the weather in the picture.

Rain falls into the open
top of the rain gauge.

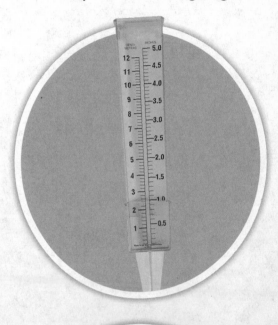

A wind vane shows the
direction the wind is
coming from.

What are the four seasons?

Circle the picture that looks most like the season outside now.

my planet diary

Fact or Fiction?

Read Together

Suppose it is winter where you live. You may think that it is winter everywhere. It is not. People in the south half of the world are out swimming at the beach. It is summer there. The seasons in the south half of the world are opposite the seasons in the north half.

Suppose it is spring where you live. **Write** what season it is in the south half of the world.

UNLOCK THE BIG ?

I will know how weather changes from season to season.

Word to Know

season

Spring

A **season** is a time of year. The four seasons are spring, summer, fall, and winter.

Spring comes after winter. Spring is warmer than winter. Days might be rainy. This helps plants grow. Many animals have babies in spring.

⊙ Sequence **Write** what season comes after winter.

Alligators lay their eggs in the spring.

221

Summer and Fall

Summer comes after spring.

Summer is warmer than spring.

Summer can be very dry.

Many plants grow in the summer.

Baby animals grow in the summer.

Fall comes after summer.

Fall is cooler than summer.

Some leaves change colors.

Some animals store food for winter.

Point to the summer picture.

Point to the fall picture.

Compare summer and fall where you live.

Write how summer and fall are alike.

Winter

Winter comes after fall.
Winter can be the coldest season.
It snows in some places.

Some plants die in winter.
Some animals grow thick fur.
The fur keeps them warm.

Tell how winter where you live is different from the picture.

Thick fur keeps the rabbit warm in winter.

How does water vapor condense?

Follow a Procedure

☑ **1.** Fill one can halfway with ice water. Fill the other can halfway with warm water.

🛑 **Be careful!** Check the cans for sharp edges. Your teacher will have used tape to cover any sharp edges.

Materials

2 cans (without sharp edges)

plastic cup with ice water

plastic cup with warm water

timer

Inquiry Skill
Scientists observe what happens and **record** their results.

☑ **2. Observe** the outside of each can. **Record** what you observe.

☑ **3.** Wait 5 minutes.

☑ **4.** What changes do you see on the outside of each can? Record.

Outside of Can		
	At Beginning	After 5 Minutes
Warm water		
Ice water		

Analyze and Conclude

5. How did the outside of the cans change?

_____

_____

_____

_____

6. **UNLOCK THE BIG ?** **Infer** How does water vapor turn into clouds?

_____

_____

_____

_____

_____

Meteorologist

Dr. J. Marshall Shepherd spent many years as a research meteorologist at NASA. He now teaches about weather.

A meteorologist is a scientist who studies or predicts the weather. Some meteorologists use special weather tools to collect data.

Some meteorologists make special maps about the weather. Meteorologists share their predictions about what the weather will be like.

Picture Clues Look at the picture of Dr. Shepherd working. **Write** what tools he uses to study the weather.

226

Vocabulary Smart Cards

evaporate
water vapor
weather
temperature
season

Play a Game!

Cut out the cards.

Work with a partner.

Pick a card.

Show your partner the front of the card.

Have your partner tell what the word means.

temperature

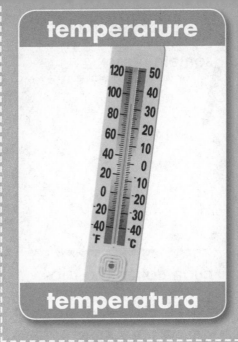

temperatura

evaporate

evaporar

season

estación

water vapor

vapor de agua

weather

tiempo

227

to change from a liquid to a gas

cambiar de líquido a gas

how hot or cold something is

cuán caliente o frío está algo

water that is a gas

agua que es gas

a time of year

período del año

what it is like outside

cómo está afuera

Chapter 6
Study Guide REVIEW THE BIG ? How can you describe weather?

 Earth Science

 **Lesson 1** What is the water cycle?

- Water becomes water vapor when it evaporates in the water cycle.

Lesson 2 What is weather?

- Weather is what it is like outside.
- You can be safe in a storm.

Lesson 3 How can you measure weather?

- You can use tools to measure weather.
- Temperature can be hot or cold.

Lesson 4 What are the four seasons?

- The four seasons are spring, summer, fall, and winter.

Chapter Review

 How can you describe weather?

Lesson 1

1. Vocabulary Fill in the blank.

Water turns into _____ when it evaporates.

2. Sequence Draw what might come next in the water cycle after clouds form.

Lesson 2

3. Vocabulary What is weather?

_____

_____

_____

4. Explain Write one way to stay safe in a hurricane.

_____

_____

_____

_____

Lesson 3

5. **Classify Draw** an ✗ on the tool you would use to measure temperature.

6. What does a rain gauge measure? **Fill in** the bubble.

Ⓐ temperature   Ⓒ amount of rain

Ⓑ wind speed   Ⓓ length

Lesson 4

7. **Describe Write** what fall is like where you live.

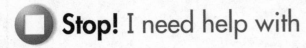

Got it?

🔲 **Stop!** I need help with
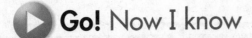

▶ **Go!** Now I know

Which soil settles first?

Materials

graduated
cylinder

gravel, sand,
and clay soil

plastic bottles
with caps

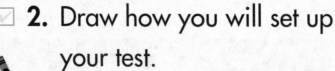

funnel and
water

Inquiry Skill
When you do
an **experiment**
you change
only one thing.

Soil can be moved by water in rivers. Find out how different soils settle out in rivers.

Ask a question.

How does soil settle out in water?

Make a prediction.

1. If soil particles are larger, they will settle
(a) faster.
(b) slower.
(c) at the same speed.

Plan a fair test.

Use the same amount of soil and water.

Design your test.

☑ **2.** Draw how you will set up
your test.

☑ **3.** List your steps.

Do your test.

☑ **4.** Follow your steps.

Collect and record data.

☑ **5.** Fill in the chart.

Tell your conclusion.

6. Compare you prediction with your results.

Make a Concept Map

- Cut out pictures of the four seasons in magazines.

- Make a concept map using words and your pictures.

- Tell what weather is like in each season where you live.

Using Scientific Methods

1. Ask a question.

2. Make a hypothesis.

3. Plan a fair test.

4. Do your test.

5. Collect and record data.

6. Tell your conclusion.

Write a Song

- Write a song about the sun.

- Tell how the sun can help people.

- Tell how the sun can hurt people.

Erosion

- Gather samples of sand, soil, and clay.

- Find out how long it takes erosion to move each one.

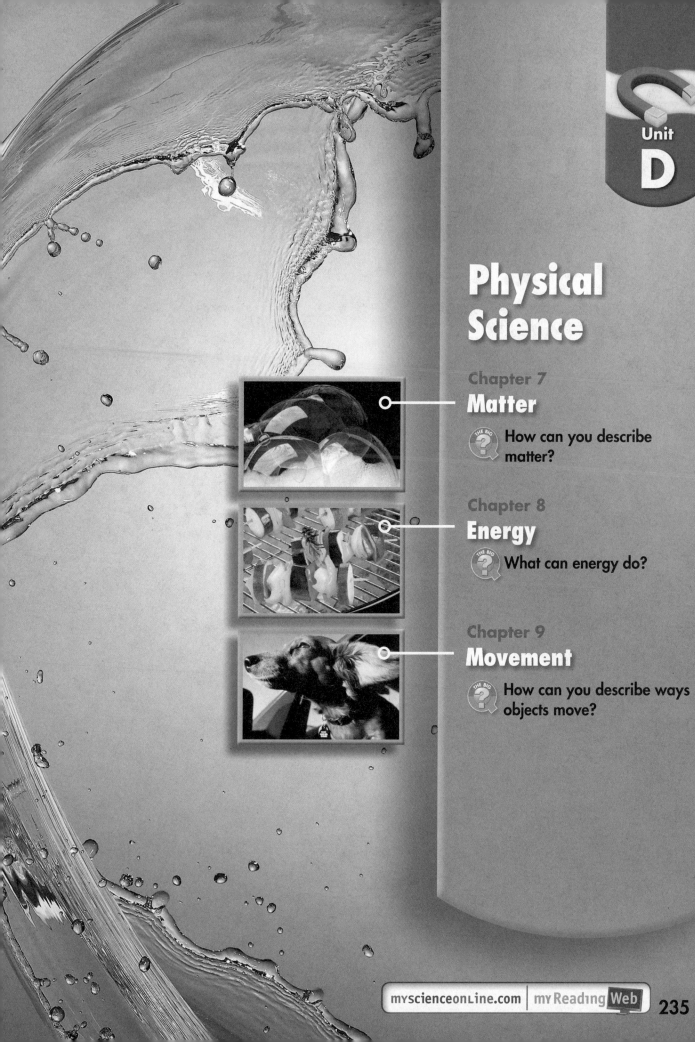

Physical Science

What is inside a bubble?

Matter

Chapter 7

Tell how you make bubbles.

 How can you describe matter?

Go to www.myscienceonline.com and click on: ⊗

UntamedScience
Go on a science adventure with the Ecogeeks!

Got it? **60-Second Video**
Watch and learn.

Explore It! Animation
Interact with the lab and see what happens!

Vocabulary Smart Cards
Hear and see your vocabulary words online!

How can you use a tool to measure?

☑ **1.** Use Straw Ruler A.

Measure the width of your desk.

How many straw pieces wide is it?

Record. Measure 3 more things.

Inquiry Skill
You can **estimate** before you measure.

☑ **2.** Use Straw Ruler B. Measure each thing again. Record.

What I Measured	Measured Using Straw Ruler A	Measured Using Straw Ruler B

Explain Your Results

3. Infer Why were your **measurements** different?

_____

_____

4. Why measure with the same size unit?

_____

_____

⊙ Main Idea and Details

The **main idea** is what the
sentences are about.
Details tell about the main idea.

A Clay Cat

The object is a clay cat.
The ears are blue triangles.
The whiskers are long and yellow.

Practice It!

Write two details that tell about the main idea.

The object is a clay cat.

Main Idea

Detail   Detail

239

What is matter?

Draw another object in the classroom.

MY PLANET DIARY

Fact or Fiction?

Pumice is a rock. Do you think it will sink or float?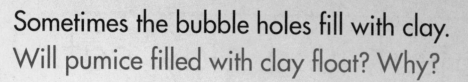

Pumice forms when lava from a volcano cools and hardens quickly. Pumice has lots of bubble holes. These holes are filled with air. The air bubbles cannot escape. Pumice floats because it is full of air bubbles.

pumice

Sometimes the bubble holes fill with clay. Will pumice filled with clay float? Why?

UNLOCK THE BIG ?

I will know how to describe matter. I will know how to group matter.

Words to Know

matter   weight

mass

Tell about the object.

Matter

Matter is anything that takes up space.

Matter has mass.

Mass is the amount of matter in an object.

The table is matter and has mass.

The table has more mass than the glue bottles.

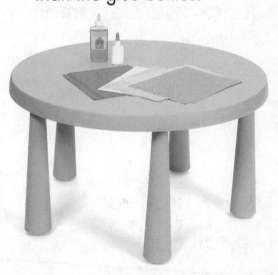

◎ **Main Idea and Details**

Write two details about matter.

Matter takes up space.

Main Idea

Detail

Detail

241

Objects and Matter

All objects are made of matter.
You can describe objects many ways.
Objects can be different colors.
Objects can be different
sizes and shapes.
Objects can be hard or soft.
The red marble is round and hard.

Label the objects.
square   purple   small

Draw an X on
two soft objects.

Describe and Group Objects

Objects can feel different.
The wall feels smooth.
Objects can be heavy or light.
Weight is how heavy an object is.
The books are heavy.

You can group objects by how
they are alike.
The balls and marbles are alike.
The balls and marbles are round.

Tell how you can sort the objects in the room by color.

Tell how you would order the orange ball, softball, and tennis ball from heavy to light. **Tell** which object has the greatest mass.

More Ways to Describe Objects

Objects can float or sink.

Float means to stay on top of a liquid.

Sink means to fall to the bottom of a liquid.

Lemonade is a liquid.

The ice cubes float in the lemonade.

Objects can be different temperatures.

The lemonade is cold.

Objects can be made of different materials.

The sink is metal.

The timer is plastic.

Draw an X on something that sinks.

Circle something that is hot.

Measure Length
Length is another way to describe objects. Use paper clips to measure your desk. How wide is it? How long is it? Do the same thing using your hand, your shoe, or cubes.

Write two words that describe the lemonade.

What are solids, liquids, and gases?

Envision It!

Draw an X on an object that is filled with a gas.

Inquiry **Explore It!**

What are the states of matter like?

☐ **1.** Gently squeeze each bag. **Observe.**

☐ **2.** Tell the shape of the rock. Tell the shape of the water and the air. **Record.**

Materials

rock in sealed plastic bag

water in sealed plastic bag

air in sealed plastic bag

Explain Your Results

3. Classify How are solids, liquids, and gases different?

UNLOCK
THE BIG
?

I will know that matter can be a solid, a liquid, or a gas.

Words to Know

| solid | liquid | gas |
| freeze | melt | boil |

Solids

Matter can be a solid, liquid, or gas.

A **solid** has its own shape.

A solid has its own size.

A solid does not change shape when it is moved.

The box is a solid.
The toys are solids.

◎ Main Idea and Details

Write two details about solids.

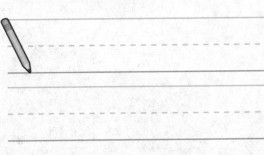

Tell what happens to the shape of a toy when you pick it up.

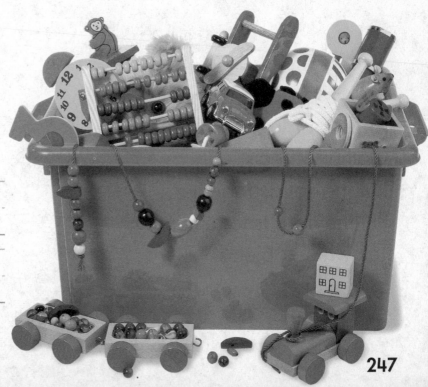

247

Liquids and Gases

A **liquid** takes the shape of its container.

You can pour a liquid.

Water is a liquid.

A **gas** can change shape and size.

A gas takes the shape of its container.

A gas fills all of its container.

You cannot see most gases.

Air is a gas.

(Circle) something that contains a liquid.

Tell one thing about each kind of matter.

At-Home Lab

Kinds of Matter
Gather objects.
Put the solids together.
Put the liquids together.
Tell which objects
contain a gas.

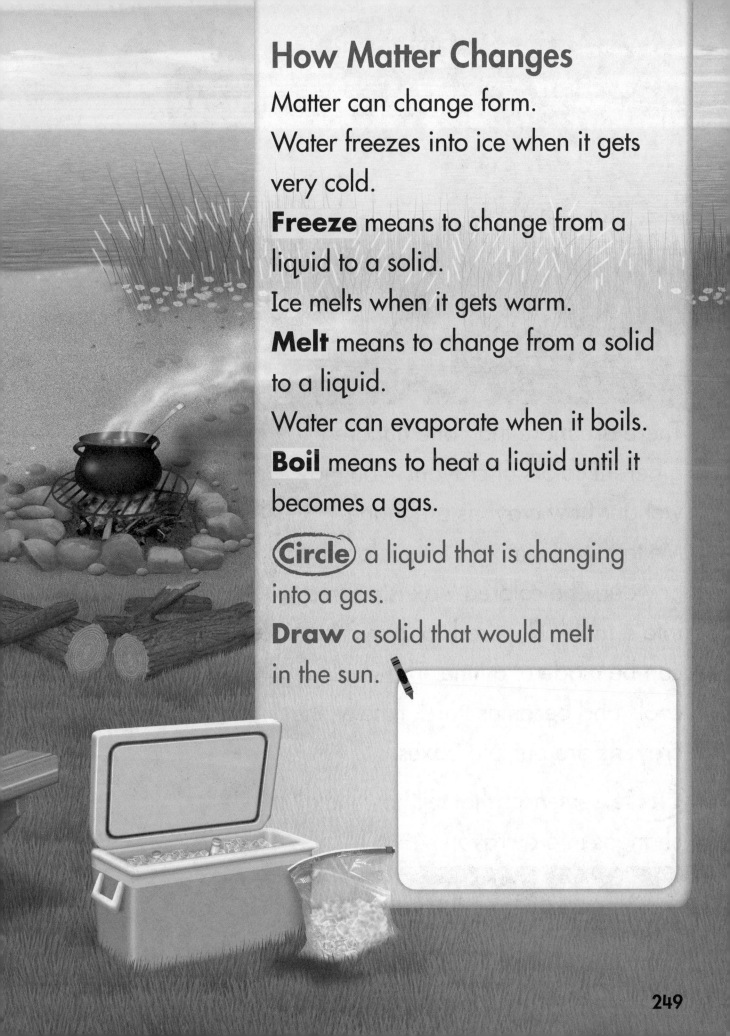

How Matter Changes

Matter can change form.

Water freezes into ice when it gets very cold.

Freeze means to change from a liquid to a solid.

Ice melts when it gets warm.

Melt means to change from a solid to a liquid.

Water can evaporate when it boils.

Boil means to heat a liquid until it becomes a gas.

(Circle) a liquid that is changing into a gas.

Draw a solid that would melt in the sun.

How can matter change?

Tell how the clay is changed.

MY PLANET DIARY Did You Know?

There are more than one hundred different colors of crayons. You may wonder how crayons are made. Melted wax is mixed with colored powder. The colored wax is poured into a mold. Hundreds of crayons can be made at a time. The wax cools and becomes hard. Finally, the crayons are put into boxes.

Circle sentences that tell how wax changes into a crayon.

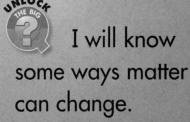
Changes in Matter

Matter can be changed.
The color of matter can change.
The size of matter can change.
The shape of matter can change.

◎ **Main Idea and Details**

Write two details about how matter can change.

Tell how the popcorn changes.

251

At-Home Lab

Objects Change
Look around your home. Find ways people change matter. Tell how they changed it.

Bend and Cut

You can bend a plastic straw.
The straw changes shape.
The straw is still made of plastic.

You can cut paper.
You can fold paper.
The paper changes shape.
The paper does not change color.
It is still paper.

Write what stays the same when you cut paper.

Different Matter

Matter can be changed
to different kinds of matter.
Wood can burn.
The wood changes color.
The wood changes to ash,
water, and gas.
It will not change back to wood.

Iron can turn into rust.
Rust is a kind of matter made
from iron and oxygen.
Oxygen is a gas in the air.
Iron is strong.
Rust breaks easily.
Rust will not change back to iron.

(Circle) two ways one kind of matter
can change to another kind of matter.

Iron might turn to rust
when it rains.

Wood changes to ash.

253

What is a mixture?

Tell what parts are mixed together.

Inquiry Explore It!

How can you separate solids and liquids?

Materials

cup with water

spoon

lemonade powder

☑ **1.** Put $\frac{1}{2}$ spoonful of lemonade powder into a cup with water. Stir. **Observe.**

☑ **2.** Wait 3 days. Observe. **Record.**

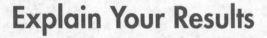

_____

- - - - - - - - - - - - - - - - - - -

_____

- - - - - - - - - - - - - - - - - - -

Explain Your Results

3. Infer How did the solid separate from the water?

_____

- - - - - - - - - - - - - - - - - - -

_____

Mixtures

You can mix matter.
A **mixture** has more than
one kind of matter.
The soup has solids and a liquid.
You can take the solids out of the liquid.
They are still the same kind of solids.
The liquid is the same too.

Chicken noodle soup
is a mixture.

Look at the picture.
Write what solids are
in the soup.

255

Kinds of Mixtures

You can mix solids with solids.
Buttons and beads are solids.
You can put them together to
make a mixture.

buttons and beads

You can mix liquids with liquids.
You can mix two juices together.
Some liquids do not mix together well.
Oil and water do not mix together well.

Tell what you think happens when
you try to mix oil and water.

oil and water

cranberry juice and
orange juice

You can mix a solid with a liquid.
Some solids dissolve in liquids.
Dissolve means to
spread throughout a liquid.
Salt will dissolve in water.
Marbles will not dissolve in water.

Underline what dissolve means.

◉ **Main Idea and Details**
Write two details about mixtures.

salt and water

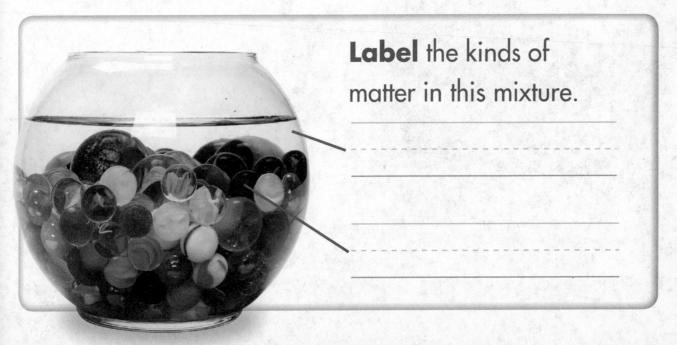

Label the kinds of
matter in this mixture.

Inquiry — Investigate It!

How are objects different?

Follow a Procedure

☑ **1. Observe**   Look at all the objects.

☑ **2. Classify**

Put the solid objects together.
Put the liquid objects together.

Materials

gram cubes

2 metal marbles

ice cube

water

milk

Inquiry Skill
To **observe** means to look carefully.

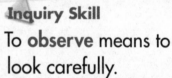

☐ **3.** Classify each object as hard or wet.
Use the chart. Make an ✕ for each object.

Observations		
	Hard	**Wet**
Gram cubes		
Metal marbles		
Ice cube		
Water		
Milk		

Analyze and Conclude

4. Draw a Conclusion How are these solids the same?
How are these liquids the same?

_____

_____

_____

5. 🔒 Which two states of matter did you **observe**?
Which did you not observe?

_____

_____

_____

_____

Matter All Around

You can learn about solids, liquids, and gases where you live. Go outside or to a park with an adult. Look around. What solids do you see? What liquids do you see? What clues do you see to know that there are gases?

Describe a solid, liquid, or gas that is outside.

What is it?	What is it like?

Vocabulary Smart Cards

matter
mass
weight
solid
liquid
gas
freeze
melt
boil
rust
mixture
dissolve

Play a Game!

Cut out the cards.

Work with a partner. Cover up the words on each card.

Look at the picture and guess the word.

261

solid

sólido

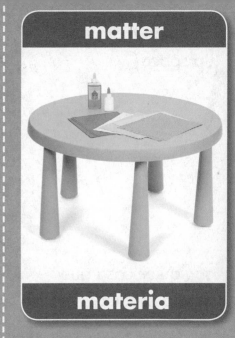

matter

materia

liquid

líquido

mass

masa

gas

gas

weight

peso

anything that takes up space

cualquier cosa que ocupa espacio

matter that has its own shape and size

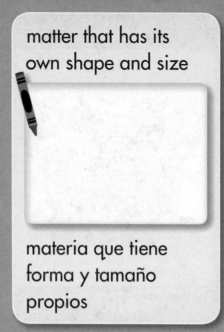

materia que tiene forma y tamaño propios

the amount of matter in an object

cantidad de materia de un objeto

matter that takes the shape of its container

materia que toma la forma del recipiente que la contiene

how heavy an object is

cuán pesado es un objeto

matter that can change size and shape

materia que puede cambiar de tamaño y forma

	rust 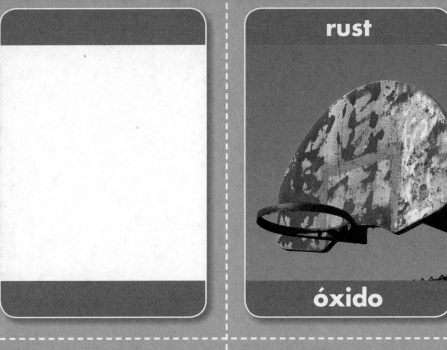 **óxido**	**freeze**  **congelar**
	mixture  **mezcla**	**melt**  **derretir**
	dissolve  **disolver**	**boil**  **hervir**

to change from a liquid to a solid	a kind of matter made from iron and oxygen	
cambiar de líquido a sólido	tipo de materia hecha de hierro y oxígeno	
to change from a solid to a liquid	more than one kind of matter	
cambiar de sólido a líquido	más de un tipo de materia	
to heat a liquid until it becomes a gas	to spread throughout a liquid	
calentar un líquido hasta que se convierte en gas	revolver completamente algo dentro de un líquido	

Study Guide

Lesson 1

What is matter?
- Matter takes up space and has mass.
- Weight is one way to describe objects.

Lesson 2

What are solids, liquids, and gases?
- Matter can be a solid, liquid, or gas.
- Water can freeze, melt, or boil.

Lesson 3

How can matter change?
- The color and size of matter can change.
- Iron can change to rust.

Lesson 4

What is a mixture?
- A mixture can have solids and liquids.
- Some solids dissolve in liquids.

Lesson 1

1. What takes up space? **Fill in** the bubble.

   Ⓐ force   Ⓒ matter

   Ⓑ speed   Ⓓ direction

2. Classify How can you group the blocks in the picture?

_____

- -

_____

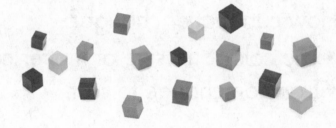

Lesson 2

3. Describe Write what a gas can do.

_____

- -

_____

4. Apply Draw three ways that water can change.

freeze	melt	boil

Lesson 3

5. Vocabulary Write about the change in the picture.

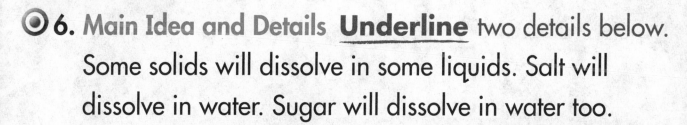

Lesson 4

⊙ **6. Main Idea and Details Underline** two details below.
Some solids will dissolve in some liquids. Salt will
dissolve in water. Sugar will dissolve in water too.

Got it?

☐ **Stop!** I need help with

▶ **Go!** Now I know

267

What makes food cook on a grill?

Energy

 Try It! What does light do?

Lesson 1 How do we use energy?

Lesson 2 What gives off heat?

Lesson 3 What is light?

Lesson 4 What is sound?

 Investigate It! What sounds can
bottles make?

Tell what you know about the coals
in the grill.

What can energy do?

Go to **www.myscienceonline.com** and click on: ⊗

UntamedScience™
Watch the Ecogeeks in this wild video.

Got *it*? 60-Second Video
Take one minute to learn science!

 Investigate It! Simulation
Quick and easy online experiments

I Will Know...
See what you've learned about science.

What does light do?

Materials
flashlight
cardboard
white paper
plastic wrap
foil wax paper

☐ **1.** Turn on the light.

☐ **2.** Shine it at the plastic wrap.

Observe.

Is the light bright?
Is the light dim?
Is there no light?

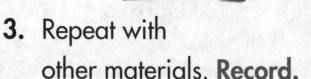

☐ **3.** Repeat with other materials. **Record.**

Inquiry Skill
After you **observe**, you can collect data.

Material	Bright Light	Dim Light	No Light

Explain Your Results

4. Observe What did the light do?

_____

⊙ Cause and Effect

A **cause** is why something happens.

An **effect** is what happens.

A Windy Day

It is a windy day.
You run across the park.
You hold your kite high.
The wind catches it.
Soon the kite flies in the sky!

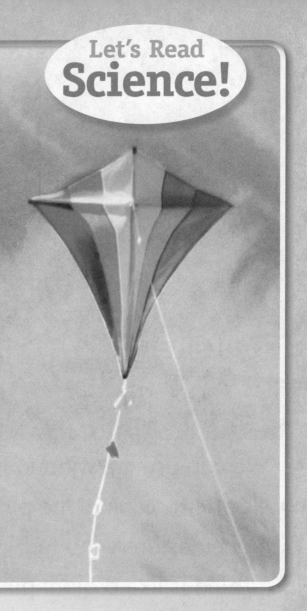

Practice It!

Write what happens when the wind catches a kite.

Cause

Effect

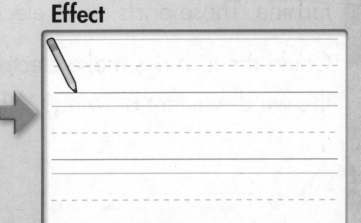

The wind catches the kite.

How do we use energy?

Tell what things in the picture use energy.

my planet diary Did You Know?

Read Together

We can use the wind to make electricity. Look at the picture. The machines are wind turbines. A wind turbine is like a giant pinwheel. The wind turns the turbine's blades. The turning blades move parts inside the turbine. These parts make electricity.

Could the turbines make electricity if the wind was not blowing? Why?

_____

_____

_____

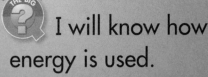
Words to Know

electricity
energy

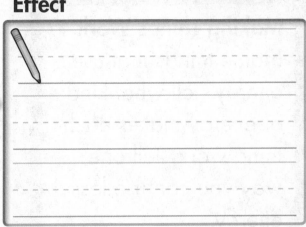

Energy

Click! You turn on the lamp.
Electricity makes the lamp glow.
The lamp will not glow without electricity.

Electricity is a kind of energy.
Energy can cause change or do work.

○ **Cause and Effect** **Write** what happens if you turn off electricity to the lamp.

Cause	Effect
The lamp has no electricity.	

273

Cars and Energy

Cars use energy.

Most cars get energy from fuel.
Some fuel is burned to make
heat or power.

Cars use gasoline for fuel.
A car's engine burns the gasoline.
The car has energy to move.

Tell what gives the car in the picture
the energy to move.

Cars get gasoline from
gas pumps.

Go Green

Making Things Work
Name things that use
energy. Tell what kind
of energy makes each
thing work. Tell one
way you can use less
energy.

Using Energy

Moving water has energy.
Moving water turns the waterwheel in the picture.

Batteries store energy.
Batteries change the stored energy to electricity.
The toy car uses electricity to move.

Wind the key.
The robot stores energy as you wind.
Let go of the key.
The robot moves.
The stored energy changes to moving energy.

Tell where the waterwheel gets energy to move.

Write where each object gets energy.

275

What gives off heat?

Draw an ✗ on what makes heat.

Inquiry **Explore It!**

How can texture affect the heat produced by rubbing?

☑ **1.** Rub 2 plastic squares together for 10 seconds. Feel them. **Record.**

☑ **2.** Repeat using the sandpaper squares.

Explain Your Results

3. Which material felt warmer? Explain.

4. Infer Does rubbing rougher materials together produce more or less heat?

Materials

2 plastic squares

2 sandpaper squares

clock with second hand

Heat from Sunlight

Heat comes from the sun.
Heat moves from warmer
places to cooler places.
Heat moves from warmer objects to
cooler objects.
Sunlight warms the land.
Sunlight warms the water.
Sunlight warms the air.

⊙ **Cause and Effect**
Write what warms the
sand at the beach.

_____

_____

The sand is warmer
on a sunny day than on
a cloudy day.

Heat from People

Heat comes from people.
Rub your hands together fast.
How do your hands feel?
Your hands feel warm.
Rubbing your hands together
makes heat.
Running makes heat too.

Tell how the children in the
picture make heat.

◉ **Cause and Effect** How can you
make heat with your hands?

Lightning Lab

Make Heat
Run in place. Keep
running for two
minutes. How do you
feel? Tell a partner.

You make heat when
you move.
You can feel the heat
when you run.

Heat from Fire

Look at the picture above.
Heat comes from the fire.
The heat warms the food.
The heat warms the air.

Draw arrows on the picture
to show how heat is moving.
List two other things that can
give off heat.

_____

_____

_____

_____

What is light?

Draw one more object that makes light.

my planeT DiaRY INVENTION!

The first electric lights did not last long. They would burn out quickly. Thomas Edison wanted a light that lasted a long time. Thomas Edison and his team worked hard. They found a material that did not burn out quickly. They used the material to make the light bulb.

Write why light bulbs are important.

_____

_____

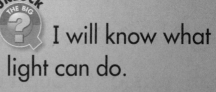
Word to Know

shadow

What Makes Light

Light is a kind of energy.
We can see light energy.
Light comes from the sun.
Light comes from other stars.
Light comes from candles.
Light comes from lamps too.

Circle where light might come from.

Look at the pictures.
Tell two more things that make light.

Fireflies make their own light.

Light Shines Through

Light passes through a window.
Light passes through thin paper.
Light will not pass through you.
You make a shadow.

A **shadow** forms when something blocks the light.

Tell why you can see the light in the lanterns.

Draw a picture of you and your shadow.

What Light Can Do

Light travels in a straight line.
Light bounces off objects that
are smooth and shiny.
Light bounces back to you from
a mirror.
That is why you can see yourself.

Cause and Effect Look at the
pictures. **Tell** how the shape of the
mirror changes what you see.

283

Lesson 4

What is sound?

Tell about the sounds these instruments make.

Inquiry **Explore It!**

How can you make sound?

☐ **1. Measure** 2 meters of string.

☐ **2.** Tie the string tight around a desk.

☐ **3.** Pluck the string.

☐ **4.** Tell what happened when you plucked the string.

Put the blocks under the string.

Materials

string

meterstick

scissors

2 blocks

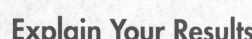

Explain Your Results

5. **Communicate** How can you change the sound?

Word to Know

vibrate

Sounds

Sound is a kind of energy.

We can hear sound energy.

Sound comes from objects that vibrate.

Vibrate means to move back and forth very fast.

The boy plucks the guitar strings.

You hear sound when the strings vibrate.

⊙ **Cause and Effect Tell** what happens when the boy plucks the guitar strings.

Tap your pencil on your desk. **Tell** what happens.

Different guitar strings make different sounds.

285

Loud and Soft

Listen to the sounds around you.

Some sounds are loud.

Some sounds are soft.

A school bell ringing is loud.

The chirp of a baby bird is soft.

(Circle) the picture below that shows something that makes a loud sound.

Draw an X on what makes a soft sound.

High and Low

Some sounds are high.
Some sounds are low.
You can sing a song in
a high voice.
You can sing a song in
a low voice.

(Circle) the picture that shows
something that makes
a low sound.

At-Home Lab

Making Sounds
Use different objects
to make sounds. List
the sounds in a chart.
Write if each sound is
high or low. Write if
each sound is loud
or soft.

What sounds can bottles make?

Follow a Procedure

☑ **1.** Blow over the top of Bottle A. Listen to the sound.

☑ **2.** Repeat Step 1 with Bottle B and Bottle C.

Materials

2 bottles with water

1 almost empty bottle

Inquiry Skill
When you **infer**, you figure something out.

288

☑ **3. Record** the sounds you hear.

Sounds from Each Bottle	
Bottle	**Sound**
A (almost empty)	
B (half full)	
C (almost full)	

Analyze and Conclude

4. Write a sentence about each sound.

_____

_____

_____

5. Infer   How did the bottles make sounds?

_____

_____

_____

Solar Power

The sun can help us make electricity. Look at the car and the house. Find the panels. These are called solar panels. Solar panels collect energy from the sun. The panels turn the energy into electricity. Solar power helps keep the air clean. This helps the environment.

Underline what solar panels do.

Circle the solar panels on the house.

Tell what is making the car work.

Vocabulary Smart Cards

electricity
energy
heat
shadow
vibrate

Play a Game!

Cut out the cards.

Work with a partner.

Pick a card.

Show your partner the front of the card.

Have your partner make a sentence about the word.

shadow

sombra

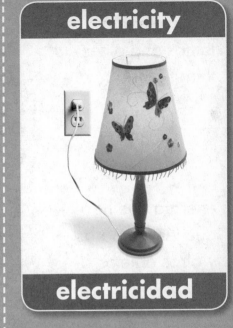

electricity

electricidad

vibrate

vibrar

energy

energía

shadow

heat

calor

energy that makes lamps and other things work

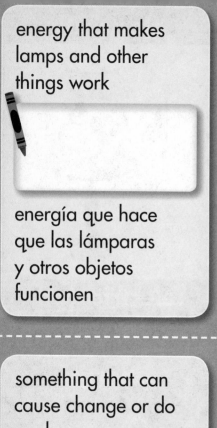

energía que hace que las lámparas y otros objetos funcionen

dark shape made when something blocks light

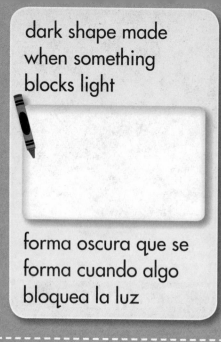

forma oscura que se forma cuando algo bloquea la luz

something that can cause change or do work

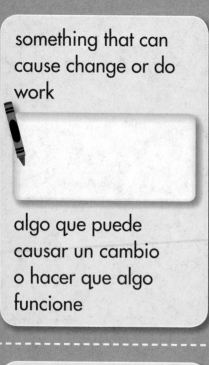

algo que puede causar un cambio o hacer que algo funcione

to move back and forth very fast

mover hacia delante y hacia atrás muy rápidamente

moves from warmer places to cooler places

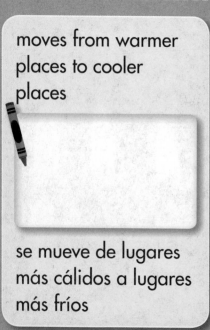

se mueve de lugares más cálidos a lugares más fríos

Study Guide

REVIEW THE BIG ? What can energy do?

Lesson 1

How is energy used?
- We use energy to make things work.
- Electricity and gasoline are kinds of energy.

Lesson 2

What gives off heat?
- Heat moves from warmer to cooler places.
- The sun and people give off heat.

Lesson 3

What is light?
- Light passes through some things.
- A shadow is made when light is blocked.

Lesson 4

What is sound?
- Sounds are made when things vibrate.
- Sounds can be loud or soft or high or low.

Lesson 1

1. **Vocabulary Draw** an X on the object that uses electricity to work.

2. **Describe Write** what energy turns a waterwheel.

Lesson 2

3. **Vocabulary Draw** two things that give off heat.

4. **Cause and Effect Write** how your hands feel when you rub them together.

Lesson 3

5. Which object will light pass through?
Fill in the bubble.

Ⓐ rock   Ⓒ window

Ⓑ mirror   Ⓓ apple

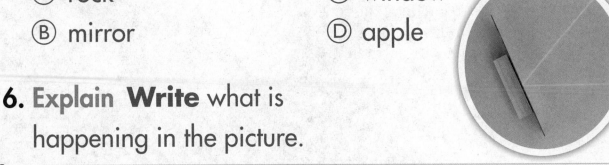

6. Explain Write what is happening in the picture.

_____

_____

Lesson 4

7. Evaluate Write whether water dripping in a sink would be loud or soft.

_____

_____

_____

Got it?

⬜ **Stop!** I need help with _____

_____

▶ **Go!** Now I know _____

Why do dogs stick their heads out of car windows?

Movement

Chapter 9

Tell what happens when the dog sticks its head out of the window.

 How can you describe ways objects move?

Go to www.myscienceonline.com and click on:
×

 Untamed Science
Sing and dance to an Ecogeek music video!

Got it? **60-Second Video**
Watch and learn.

Envision It!
See what you already know about science.

 my planet diary
Did you know? Find out through Planet Diary.

How can you make a toy move?

☐ **1.** Pick a toy. Make it move. **Observe.**

☐ **2.** Make the toy move a different way.

Explain Your Results

3. Communicate Write two ways you made the toy move.

I _____ the toy.

I _____ the toy.

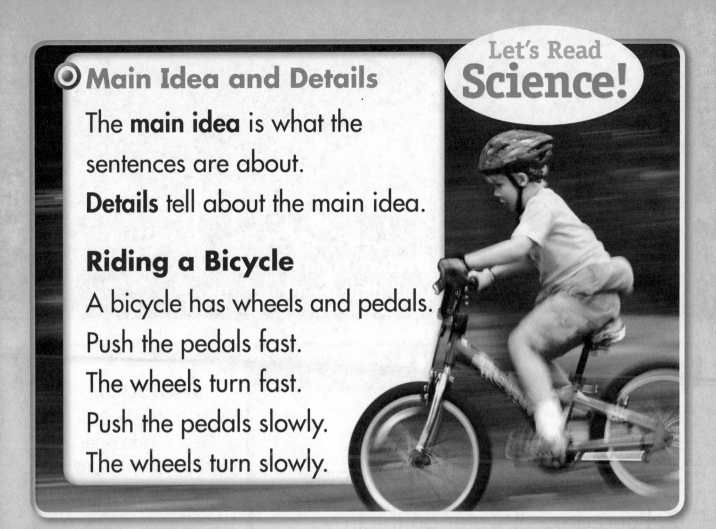

◉ Main Idea and Details

The **main idea** is what the sentences are about.

Details tell about the main idea.

Riding a Bicycle

A bicycle has wheels and pedals.
Push the pedals fast.
The wheels turn fast.
Push the pedals slowly.
The wheels turn slowly.

Practice It!

Write two details that tell about the main idea.

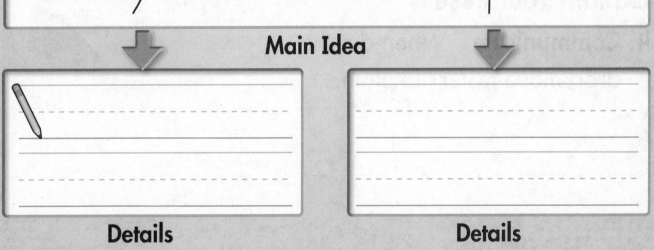

A bicycle has wheels and pedals.

Main Idea

Details   Details

How can objects move?

Draw a line to show how you think the objects move.

 **Inquiry** **Explore It!**

How can water move?

☐ **1.** Put one end of a tray on 2 books.

☐ **2.** Put a drop of water on the tray. **Observe** how the drop moves.

☐ **3.** Add 2 more books. Repeat.

Materials

 plastic dropper

plastic cup with water

4 books

tray with waxed paper

Explain Your Results

4. Communicate When did the drop move faster? Explain.

_____

_____

_____

UNLOCK THE BIG ? I will know different ways objects can move. I will know objects move fast and slow.

Word to Know

speed

Ways to Move

Objects can move in many ways.
Objects can move in a straight line.
A car can move in a straight line.
Objects can move in a curved line.
The roller coaster moves
in a curved line.

Objects can move round
and round in a circle.
A merry-go-round moves
round and round.

⊙ **Main Idea and Details**
Underline the main idea above.

Tell how the people on the slide move.

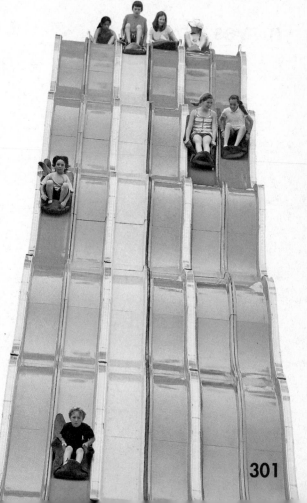

More Ways to Move

Objects can start to move.

Objects can roll.

Objects can slide.

Objects can move back and forth.

Some objects move in a zigzag.

Speed is how quickly or slowly an object moves.

Some objects move fast.

Some objects move slowly.

Objects can stop.

Draw an object that moves slowly.

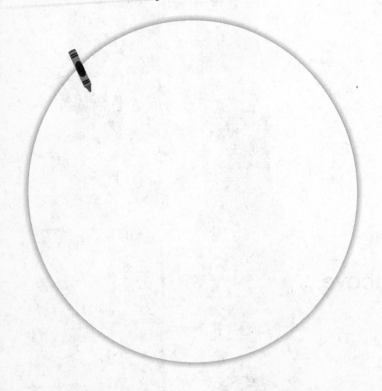

Label the objects.
fast   roll   slide

_____

_____

_____

_____

_____

On the Move
Pick a way to move. Show how you can move that way. Have a partner tell how you moved. Take turns.

Draw a line to show how the people walk across the bridge.

The people walk in a zigzag across the bridge.

303

Lesson 2

What is a force?

The dogs pull the sled.

Inquiry **Explore It!**

What makes the toy car move?

Materials

safety goggles

2 unsharpened pencils

rubber band

toy car

☐ **1.** Work together. Hold the pencils. Pull back the rubber band.

☐ **2.** Let the rubber band go. **Observe.**

Explain Your Results

Be careful! Wear safety goggles.

3. What made the car move?

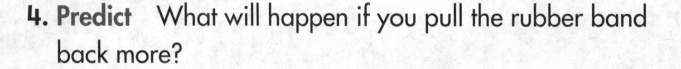

4. Predict What will happen if you pull the rubber band back more?

304

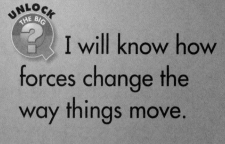

Draw an object you pull.

Word to Know

force

Force

A **force** is a push or a pull.
You use forces every day.
You pull a drawer open.
You push a drawer closed.

Draw an X in the box to show if
the picture shows a push or a pull.

Object	Push	Pull

What a Force Can Do

A force can change how objects move.

A force can start an object moving.

A force can stop a moving object.

A force can change the direction of a moving object.

⊙ **Main Idea and Details** **Write** two details about what a force can do.

The children can stop the ball from moving.

More Force, Less Force

Motion is the act of moving.

Use more force.

The motion of an object changes more.

Use less force.

The motion of an object changes less.

Tell how you can change
the motion of a bike more.

Underline how you can change
the motion of an object less.

The children kick the
ball with a lot of force.
The ball moves fast.

At-Home Lab

Roll Away
Push a ball hard.
See how far it goes.
Push a ball softly.
See how far it goes.

What is a magnet?

Circle the objects that a magnet could pull.

my planet diary Did You Know?

Think of the different things magnets can pull. Did you think of cereal? Iron is added to some cereals. Iron is a nutrient. Some cereal flakes have a lot of iron. Crush the cereal flakes. A strong magnet can pull out pieces of cereal with iron.

Write why you think cereal makers add iron to cereals.

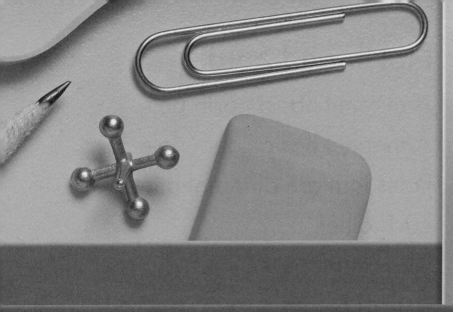

Words to Know

magnet   repel
attract

Magnets

A **magnet** is an object that attracts some metals.

Attract means to pull toward.

Magnets attract paper clips.
Paper clips are metal.
Magnets will not attract wood.
Magnets will not attract plastic.
Wood and plastic are not metals.

Magnets attract objects made of iron and steel. Iron and steel are kinds of metals. A paper clip is made of steel.

◉ **Main Idea and Details**

Underline the main idea about the magnet.

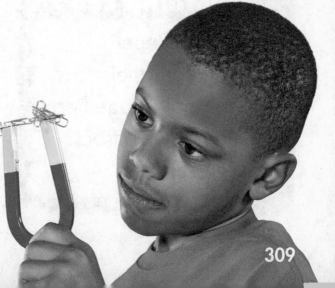

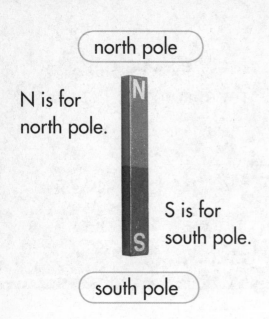

north pole

N is for north pole.

S is for south pole.

south pole

North and South

A magnet has a north pole.

A magnet has a south pole.

Poles that are different attract each other.

Poles that are alike repel each other.

Repel means to push away.

Draw what will happen if two south poles are put together.

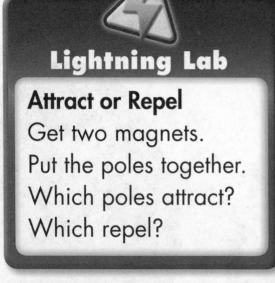

310

Near and Far

Put a magnet near a paper clip.
The magnet can pull the paper clip
without touching it.
Move the magnet far away.
The magnet cannot pull the paper clip.

Magnets can pull through thin objects
more easily than through thick objects.

Draw an X on the objects the magnets
can easily pull through.

Tell a partner why you
chose these objects.

What is gravity?

Tell which way the water moves.

Inquiry **Explore It!**

Why do things fall?

 **1.** Put a paper clip on a desk.

2. Predict What will happen if you push it off?

3. Test your prediction. **Observe.**

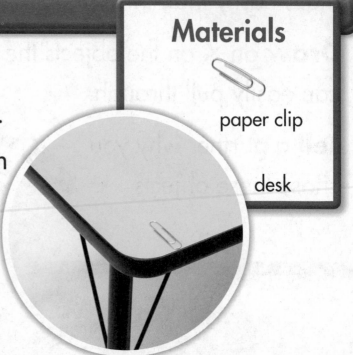

Materials

paper clip

desk

Explain Your Results

4. Explain what you **observed.**

_____

_____

_____

_____

UNLOCK THE BIG ?
I will know that gravity pulls objects toward Earth without touching them.

Word to Know

gravity

Pull of Gravity

All objects are pulled
toward Earth.
This pull is called **gravity.**
Gravity is a force.
Gravity pulls objects on or near
Earth toward it.
Gravity keeps you on the ground.
Gravity keeps your desk on
the floor.

◉ **Cause and Effect Write** what will
happen to the soccer ball next.

313

Hold Up

Gravity pulls objects toward Earth unless something holds them up. Gravity pulls on the kite. The wind holds up the kite. Gravity pulls on the roll of string. The boy holds up the roll of string.

Underline the sentence that tells why the kite stays up.

At-Home Lab

Gravity and Air
Get two sheets of paper. Make one sheet into a ball. Hold it in one hand. Hold the second sheet in your other hand. Drop them at the same time. Tell what happens.

Pull Down

Gravity can pull objects without touching them. The water shoots out of the fountain. Nothing holds the water up. Gravity pulls the water down without touching it.

Draw an arrow to show what happens to the kite when the wind stops holding it up.

How do objects move?

Follow a Procedure

☐ **1.** Drop a marble in a curved tube.

☐ **2.** **Measure** how far the marble rolls out. **Record.**

☐ **3.** Make the tube straight. Drop the marble in the tube.

☐ **4.** Measure and record.

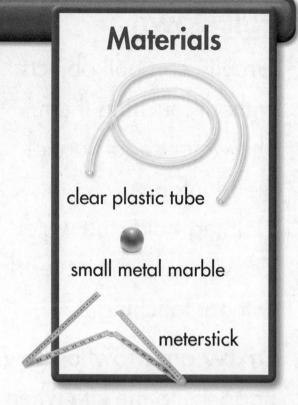

Materials

clear plastic tube

small metal marble

meterstick

Inquiry Skill
You can record to show what you **measure.**

Gravity pulls the marble down.
The tube makes the ball curve.

Distance Rolled

Shape of Tube	How far did the marble roll? (cm)
Curved	
Straight	

Analyze and Conclude

5. Draw a Conclusion Fill in the blank.

The ball rolled farther in the _____ tube.

6. 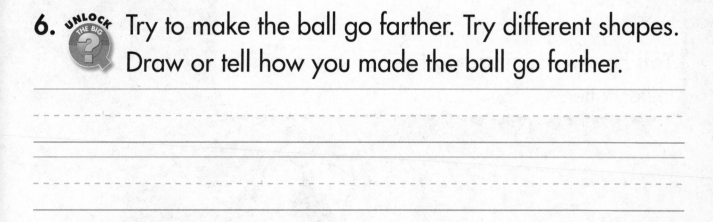 Try to make the ball go farther. Try different shapes. Draw or tell how you made the ball go farther.

Playgrounds

Playgrounds are a lot of fun. There are many ways to move at a playground.

You can slide down a slide. Some slides are curvy. You slide in a curved line. Some slides are straight. You slide in a straight line.

You move back and forth on a swing. The harder someone pushes you, the higher you go.

Write about another way you can move on a playground.

_____

- -

_____

Tell how you can use pushes to move a teeter-totter.

Vocabulary Smart Cards

speed
force
magnet
attract
repel
gravity

Play a Game!

Cut out the cards.

Work with a partner.

Pick a card.

Show your partner the front of the card.

Have your partner tell what the word means.

attract

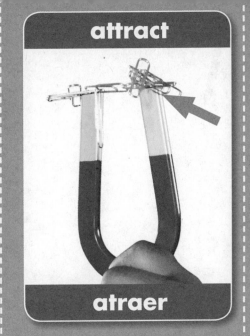

atraer

speed

rapidez

repel

repeler

force

fuerza

gravity

gravedad

magnet

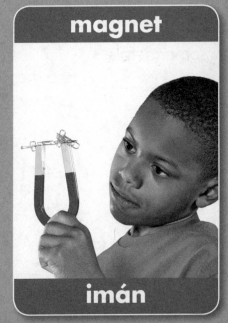

imán

how quickly or slowly
an object moves

qué tan rápido
o tan despacio
se mueve algo

to pull toward

jalar

a push or a pull

empujón o jalón

to push away

apartar

an object that attracts
some metals

objeto que atrae
algunos metales

a force that pulls
objects toward Earth

la fuerza que jala
los objetos hacia la
Tierra

320

Lesson 1

How can objects move?

- Objects can move in many different ways.
- Objects can move at different speeds.

Lesson 2

What is a force?

- A force can move an object.
- A force can change how an object moves.

Lesson 3

What is a magnet?

- A magnet attracts iron and steel.
- Poles that are alike repel each other.

Lesson 4

What is gravity?

- Gravity pulls objects toward Earth.
- Gravity pulls objects without touching them.

Lesson 1

1. Vocabulary What is speed?

_____

- -

_____

2. Apply Draw a line to show each way of moving.

| zigzag | straight | round and round |

Lesson 2

3. Apply Write one way you use a force.

_____

- -

_____

◉ **4. Main Idea and Details**
Underline two details below.
The hockey player moves the puck
in many ways. The player hits the
puck hard. The puck moves fast.

Lesson 3

5. Which object can a magnet pull? **Fill in** the bubble.

Ⓐ rubber eraser   Ⓒ wood block

Ⓑ metal paper clip   Ⓓ plastic toy

Lesson 4

6. Predict Draw what will happen next.

Got it?

◻ **Stop!** I need help with _____

_____

▶ **Go!** Now I know _____

_____

What affects how far a marble rolls?

Materials

2 metal marbles

6 books

2 metric rulers with grooves

meterstick

Ask a question.

How does ramp height affect how far a marble rolls?

Make a prediction.

1. Will a marble roll farther from a high or low ramp?

(a) high ramp

(b) low ramp

Plan a fair test.

Use two marbles that are the same.

Use two rulers that are the same.

Design your test.

☑ **2.** Draw how you will set up the test.

Inquiry Skill
You **control variables** when you change only one thing in your test.

☑ **3.** Write your steps.

Do your test.

☑ **4.** Follow your steps.

Collect and record data.

☑ **5.** Fill in the chart.

Tell your conclusion.

6. Communicate How does ramp height affect how distance rolled?

Push	Pull

Using Scientific Methods

1. Ask a question.

2. Make a hypothesis.

3. Plan a fair test.

4. Do your test.

5. Collect and record data.

6. Tell your conclusion.

Make a Poster

- Find pictures of someone pushing and pulling objects.

- Cut out the pictures. Glue the pictures of pushes on one part of the poster. Glue the pictures of pulls on the other part.

- Tell about the pictures.

Cool a Balloon

- Blow up a balloon.

- Find out if the size of the balloon changes when it is in cold water.

Write a Story

- Write a story about how an object moves.

- Write about the speed of the object and what makes the object move.

Measurements

Metric and Customary Measurements

Science uses the metric system to measure things.
Metric measurement is used around the world.
Here is how different metric measurements
compare to customary measurements.

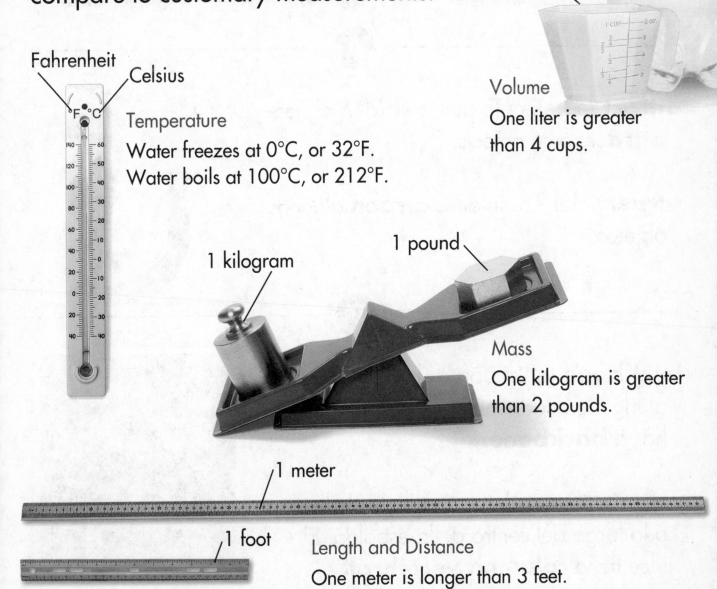

1 liter

1 cup

Volume
One liter is greater
than 4 cups.

Fahrenheit
Celsius

Temperature
Water freezes at 0°C, or 32°F.
Water boils at 100°C, or 212°F.

1 kilogram

1 pound

Mass
One kilogram is greater
than 2 pounds.

1 meter

1 foot

Length and Distance
One meter is longer than 3 feet.

Glossary

The glossary uses letters and signs to show how words are pronounced. The mark ′ is placed after a syllable with a primary or heavy accent. The mark ′ is placed after a syllable with a secondary or lighter accent.

To hear these vocabulary words and definitions, you can refer to the AudioText CD, or log on to the digital path's Vocabulary Smart Cards.

Pronunciation Key

a in hat	ō in open	sh in she
ā in age	ȯ in all	th in thin
â in care	ô in order	ᵺ in then
ä in far	oi in oil	zh in measure
e in let	ou in out	ə = a in about
ē in equal	u in cup	ə = e in taken
ėr in term	ù in put	ə = i in pencil
i in it	ü in rule	ə = o in lemon
ī in ice	ch in child	ə = u in circus
o in hot	ng in long	

A

attract (ə trakt′) To pull toward. Magnets **attract** some objects.

atraer Jalar. Los imanes **atraen** algunos objetos.

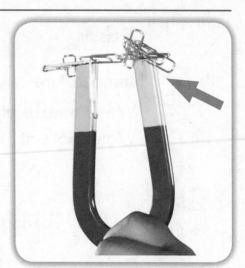

B

backbone (bak′ bōn′) The set of bones along the middle of the back. A moose has a **backbone.**

columna vertebral Conjunto de huesos a lo largo del centro de la espalda. El alce tiene **columna vertebral.**

boil (boil) To heat a liquid until it becomes a gas. The soup began to **boil** after placing it on the fire.

hervir Calentar un líquido hasta que se convierte en gas. La sopa empezó a **hervir** después de ponerla al fuego.

D

data (dā′ tə) Information you collect. You can record **data** about animals.

datos Información que reúnes. Puedes anotar **datos** acerca de los animales.

desert (dez′ ərt) Environment that is very dry. Many plants and animals live in the **desert.**

desierto Medio ambiente que es muy seco. En el **desierto** viven muchas plantas y animales diferentes.

dissolve (di zolv′) Spread throughout a liquid. Salt will **dissolve** in water.

disolver Revolver completamente algo dentro de un líquido. La sal se puede **disolver** en agua.

E

electricity (i lek′ tris′ ə tē) Energy that makes lamps and other things work. The lamp uses **electricity** to work.

electridad Energía que hace que las lámparas y otros objetos funcionen. La lámpara usa **electricidad** para poder funcionar.

energy (en′ ər jē) Something that can cause change or do work. The buildings and the car use **energy.**

energía Algo que puede causar un cambio o hacer que algo funcione. Los edificios y los carros usan **energía.**

environment (en vī′ rən mənt) All living and nonliving things in one place. Animals, plants, and rocks are part of an **environment.**

medio ambiente Todos los seres vivos y las cosas sin vida que hay en un lugar. Animales, plantas y rocas son parte de un medio **ambiente.**

erosion (i rō′ zhən) When wind or water moves rocks and soil. **Erosion** washed away the sand near the ocean.

erosión Cuando el viento o el agua mueve rocas y suelo. La **erosión** arrastró la arena cerca del mar.

evaporate (i vap′ ə rāt) To change from a liquid to a gas. The water on the sidewalk began to **evaporate.**

evaporar Cambiar de líquido a gas. El agua que había en la acera empezó a **evaporarse.**

extinct (ek stingkt′) No longer live on Earth. This sparrow is **extinct.**

extinto No vive más en la Tierra. Este gorrión está **extinto.**

F

force (fôrs) A push or a pull. The boy uses **force** to move the cart.

fuerza Empujón o jalón. El niño usa **fuerza** para mover el carro.

forest (fôr′ ist) Land that has many trees and other plants. Some bears live in the **forest.**

bosque Tierra que tiene muchos árboles y otras plantas. Algunos osos viven en el **bosque.**

fossil (fos′ əl) A print or part of a plant or animal that lived long ago. The scientist found a plant **fossil.**

fósil Huella o parte de una planta o animal que vivió hace mucho tiempo. El científico encontró una planta **fósil.**

freeze (frēz) To change from a liquid to a solid. We let water **freeze** to make ice cubes.

congelar Cambiar de líquido a sólido. Dejamos **congelar** el agua para hacer cubitos de hielo.

G

gas (gas) Matter that can change size and shape. The beach toys were full of **gas.**

gas Materia que puede cambiar de tamaño y forma. Los juguetes de playa estaban llenos de **gas.**

goal (gōl) Something you want to do. You have a **goal** to build shelter for the duck.

objetivo Algo que quieres hacer. Tu **objetivo** es construir un albergue para el pato.

gravity (grav′ ə tē) A force that pulls objects toward Earth. **Gravity** pulls the ball toward the ground.

gravedad La fuerza que jala los objetos hacia la Tierra. La **gravedad** jala la pelota hacia el piso.

H

heat (hēt) Moves from warmer places to cooler places. The **heat** from the flame melts the candles.

calor Se mueve de lugares más cálidos a lugares más fríos. El **calor** de la llama derrite las velas.

herd (hėrd) A group of animals of one kind that stay together. The **herd** of giraffes travels together.

manada Grupo de animales del mismo tipo que están juntos. Las jirafas de esa **manada** viajan juntas.

humus (hyü′ məs) Small bits of dead plants and animals in soil. Grandmother adds **humus** to the soil to help her plants grow.

humus Restos de plantas y animales muertos en el suelo. Mi abuela le añade **humus** al suelo para ayudar a sus plantas a crecer.

I

inquiry (in kwī′ rē) Looking for answers. You can use **inquiry** to learn about kinds of plants.

indagación Buscar respuestas. Puedes hacer una **indagación** para aprender sobre los tipos de plantas.

investigate (in ves′ tə gāt) To look for answers to questions. Scientists **investigate** to learn about plants.

investigar Buscar respuestas a las preguntas. Los científicos **investigan** para saber más sobre las plantas.

L

leaf (lēf) The part of a plant that makes food. A **leaf** fell from the rose bush.

hoja La parte de la planta que produce el alimento. Una **hoja** cayó del rosal de mi jardín.

life cycle (līf sī′ kəl) The way a living thing grows and changes. The **life cycle** of a tree includes a seed, a seedling, and a grown tree.

ciclo de vida Manera en que un ser vivo crece y cambia. El **ciclo de vida** de un árbol incluye la semilla, la plántula y el árbol adulto.

liquid (lik′ wid) Matter that takes the shape of its container. My mother poured the **liquid** into the glasses.

líquido Materia que toma la forma del recipiente que la contiene. Mi mamá puso el **líquido** en los vasos.

living (liv′ ing) Things that can grow and change. The tiger is a **living** thing.

vivo Seres que pueden crecer y cambiar. El tigre es un ser **vivo.**

magnet (mag′ nit) An object that attracts some metals. I picked up the paper clips with the **magnet.**

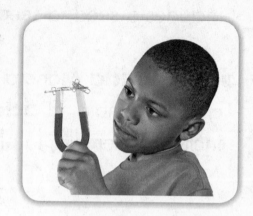

imán Objeto que atrae algunos metales. Recogí los clips con el **imán.**

mass (mas) The amount of matter in an object. The table has **mass.**

masa Cantidad de materia de un objeto. La **mesa** tiene masa.

matter (mat′ər) Anything that takes up space. Everything around you is made of **matter.**

materia Cualquier cosa que ocupa espacio. Todo lo que hay a nuestro alrededor está hecho de **materia.**

measure (mezh′ ər) To use a tool to find the size or amount of something. You can use a ruler to **measure** how long something is.

medir Usar un instrumento para saber el tamaño o la cantidad de algo. Puedes usar una regla para **medir** el largo de un objeto.

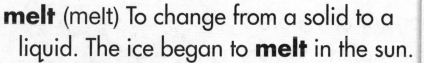

melt (melt) To change from a solid to a liquid. The ice began to **melt** in the sun.

derretir Cambiar de sólido a líquido. El hielo empezó a **derretirse** bajo el sol.

mixture (miks′ chər) More than one kind of matter. The carrots, broth, and noodles form a **mixture.**

mezcla Más de un tipo de materia. Las zanahorias, el caldo y los fideos forman una **mezcla.**

natural (nach′ ər əl) Not made by people. Fruit and wood are **natural.**

natural No hecho por las personas. Las frutas y la madera son **naturales.**

natural resource (nach′ ər əl ri sôrs′) A useful material found in nature. Water is a **natural resource.**

recurso natural Material útil que se encuentra en la naturaleza. El agua es un **recurso natural.**

need (nēd) Something a living thing must have to live. Plants grow when their **needs** are met.

necesidad Algo que un ser vivo necesita para vivir. Las plantas crecen cuando se satifacen sus **necesidades.**

nonliving (non liv′ ing) Things that do not grow and change on their own. Toys are **nonliving** things.

sin vida Cosas que no crecen y que no cambian por sí mismas. Los juguetes son cosas **sin vida.**

nutrients (nü′ trē ənts) Materials that living things need. Plants need **nutrients** to change and grow.

nutrientes Sustancias que los seres vivos necesitan. Las plantas necesitan **nutrientes** para cambiar y crecer.

nymph (nimf) A kind of young insect. A grasshopper **nymph** does not have wings.

ninfa Tipo de insecto joven. La **ninfa** del saltamontes no tiene alas.

observe (əb sėrv′) When you use your senses. You can **observe** sounds that an animal makes.

observar Cuando usas tus sentidos. Puedes **observar** los sonidos que hace un animal.

ocean (ō′ shən) Environment that is a large body of salty water. Some fish live in an **ocean** environment.

océano Medio ambiente que es un gran cuerpo de agua salada. El medio ambiente donde viven algunos peces es el **océano.**

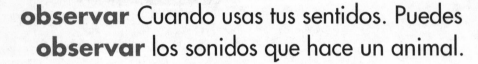

P

parent (per′ ənt) A living thing that has young. The calf needs its parent to take care of it.

progenitor Ser vivo que tiene crías. El becerro necesita que su progenitor lo cuide.

prairie (prâr′ ē) Environment that is covered with grasses. Some gophers live on **prairies.**

pradera Medio ambiente cubierto de pasto. Algunas tuzas viven en las **praderas.**

record (ri kôrd′) When scientists write or draw what they learn. It is important to **record** information during experiments.

Favorite Animals				
cat				
dog				
bird				

registrar Cuando los científicos escriben o dibujan lo que descubren. Es importante **registrar** la información durante un experimento.

recycle (rē sī′ kəl) Make used materials into new materials. You can **recycle** milk jugs.

reciclar Convertir materiales usados en materiales nuevos. Se pueden **reciclar** las jarras de leche.

reduce (ri düs′) Use less. You can **reduce** how much electricity you use.

reducir Usar menos. Se puede **reducir** la cantidad de electricidad que usamos.

repel (ri pel′) To push away. The north poles of two magnets placed together will **repel** each other.

repeler Apartar. Los polos norte de dos imanes se **repelen** si los acercan.

reuse (rē yüz′) Use again. You can **reuse** a bottle.

reutilizar Volver a usar. Se pueden **reutilizar** las botellas.

root (rüt) The part of a plant that takes in water. We covered the **roots** of the rose plant with soil.

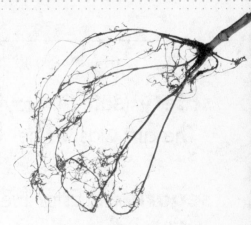

raíz La parte de la planta que toma el agua. Cubrimos las **raíces** del rosal con tierra.

rotation (rō tā′ shən) One spin around. Earth makes one **rotation** each day.

rotación Dar una vuelta sobre sí mismo. La Tierra hace una **rotación** cada día.

rust (rust) A kind of matter made from iron and oxygen. **Rust** breaks easily.

óxido Tipo de materia hecha de hierro y oxígeno. Es fácil que salga **óxido.**

safety (sāf′ tē) Staying out of danger. The girl washes her hands to stay **safe.**

seguridad Estar fuera de peligro. La niña se lava las manos para mantenerse **segura.**

season (sē′zn) A time of year. Spring is my favorite **season.**

estación Período del año. La primavera es mi **estación** favorita.

seedling (sēd′ ling) A very young plant. Rafe planted the **seedling** of an oak tree.

plántula Planta muy joven. Rafe sembró una **plántula** de roble.

shadow (shad′ō) Dark shape made when something blocks light. The boy made a **shadow** on the ground.

sombra Forma oscura que se forma cuando algo bloquea la luz. El niño produjo una **sombra** en el suelo.

shelter (shel′ tər) A safe place. The beaver uses sticks and mud for **shelter.**

albergue Lugar seguro. El castor usa palitos y lodo para su **albergue.**

soil (soil) The top layer of Earth. You can find rocks in **soil.**

suelo La capa superior de la Tierra. Puedes hallar rocas en el **suelo.**

solid (sol′ id) Matter that has its own shape and size. Each toy in the box is a **solid.**

sólido Materia que tiene forma y tamaño propios. Todos los juguetes de la caja son **sólidos.**

solution (sə lü′ shən) Something that solves a problem. The shelter is a **solution.**

solución Algo que resuelve un problema. El albergue es una **solución.**

speed (spēd) How quickly or slowly an object moves. The roller coaster moved at a very fast **speed.**

rapidez Qué tan rápido o tan despacio se mueve algo. La montaña rusa se movió con gran **rapidez.**

stem (stem) The part of a plant that takes water from the roots to the leaves. The rose's **stem** has sharp thorns.

tallo La parte de una planta que lleva el agua de las raíces a las hojas. El **tallo** del rosal tiene espinas afiladas.

sun (sun) A big ball of hot gas. The light from the **sun** warms Earth.

Sol Bola muy grande de gas caliente. La luz del **Sol** calienta la Tierra.

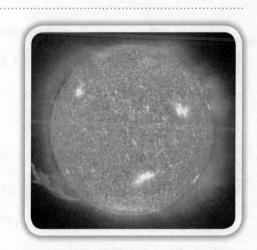

T

technology (tek nol′ ə jē) Using science to help solve problems. A computer is **technology.**

tecnología Usar las ciencias para resolver problemas. Una computadora es **tecnología.**

temperature (tem′ per ə chər) How hot or cold something is. It was hot today, and the **temperature** outside was very high.

temperatura Cuán caliente o frío está algo. Hoy la **temperatura** al aire libre estuvo muy alta.

tool (tül) Something that makes work easier. A hand lens is a **tool** that helps you see things.

instrumento Algo que hace más fácil el trabajo. Una lupa es un **instrumento** que te ayuda a ver cosas.

vibrate (vī′ brāt) To move back and forth very fast. Sound happens when objects **vibrate.**

vibrar Mover hacia delante y hacia atrás muy rápidamente. El sonido se produce cuando los objetos **vibran.**

water vapor (wȯ′ tər vā′ pər) Water that is a gas. When liquid water evaporates, it changes to a gas called **water vapor.**

vapor de agua Agua que es gas. Cuando se evapora el agua líquida, se convierte en un gas llamado **vapor de agua.**

weather (weŦH′ ər) What it is like outside. I like to drink hot chocolate when the **weather** outside is cold.

tiempo Cómo está afuera. Me gusta tomar chocolate caliente cuando el **tiempo** es frío.

weathering (we͟FH′ ər ing)) When water or ice breaks down rocks. **Weathering** can change the shape, size, and color of rocks.

meteorización Cuando el agua o el hielo rompe las rocas. La **meteorización** puede cambiar la forma, el tamaño y el color de las rocas.

weight (wāt) How heavy an object is. You can measure the **weight** of an object.

peso Cuán pesado es un objeto. Puedes medir el **peso** de un objeto.

wetland (wet′ land′) Environment that is covered with water. Tanya saw a blue heron when she visited the **wetland** near her home.

pantanal Medio ambiente cubierto de agua. Tanya vio una garza ceniza cuando fue al **pantanal** que queda cerca de su casa.

Index

Credits

Staff Credits

The people who made up the *Interactive Science* team—representing core design digital and multimedia production services, digital product development, editorial, manufacturing, and production—are listed below.

Geri Amani, Alisa Anderson, Jose Arrendondo, Amy Austin, Lindsay Bellino, Charlie Bink, Bridget Binstock, Holly Blessen, Robin Bobo, Craig Bottomley, Jim Brady, Laura Brancky, Chris Budzisz, Mary Chingwa, Sitha Chhor, Caroline Chung, Margaret Clampitt, Karen Corliss, Brandon Cole, Mitch Coulter, AnnMarie Coyne, Fran Curran, Dana Damiano, Nancy Duffner, Amanda Ferguson, David Gall, Mark Geyer, Amy Goodwin, Gerardine Griffin, Chris Haggerty, Laura Hancko, Jericho Hernandez, Autumn Hickenlooper, Guy Huff, George Jacobson, Marian Jones, Kathi Kalina, Chris Kammer, Sheila Kanitsch, Alyse Kondrat, Mary Kramer, Thea Limpus, Dominique Mariano, Lori McGuire, Melinda Medina, Angelina Mendez, Claudi Mimo, John Moore, Phoebe Novak, Anthony Nuccio, Jeffrey Osier, Julianne Regnier, Charlene Rimsa, Rebecca Roberts, Camille Salerno, Manuel Sanchez, Carol Schmitz, Amanda Seldera, Sheetal Shah, Jeannine Shelton El, Geri Shulman, Greg Sorenson, Samantha Sparkman, Mindy Spelius, Karen Stockwell, Dee Sunday, Dennis Tarwood, Jennie Teece, Lois Teesdale, Michaela Tudela, Oscar Vera, Dave Wade, Tom Wickland, James Yagelski, Tim Yetzina, Diane Zimmermann

Illustrations

xii, 96, 107, 124, 128, 210, 227, 261, 263, EM3 Precision Graphics; **146** Alan Barnard; **187** Hana C. Ichinose; **193, 199** Henk Dawson
All other illustrations Chandler Digital Art

Photographs

Every effort has been made to secure permission and provide appropriate credit for photographic material. The publisher deeply regrets any omission and pledges to correct errors called to its attention in subsequent editions.

Unless otherwise acknowledged, all photographs are the property of Pearson Education, Inc.

Photo locators denoted as follows: Top (T), Center (C), Bottom (B), Left (L), Right (R), Background (Bkgd)

COVER: Jarvell Jardey/Alamy

iv Thinkstock; **vi** ©Radius Images/Alamy; **vii** ©Masterfile Royalty-Free; **viii** (CR) ©imagebroker/Alamy Images; **ix** (CR) Melinda Fawver/Shutterstock; **x** (CR) ©Maridav/Shutterstock; **xi** (CR) ©AP Images; **xiii** (CR) ©Cliff LeSergent/Alamy; **xiv** Thinkstock; **1** (CB) ©Lisette Le Bon/SuperStock, (Bkgrd) ©niderlander/Shutterstock, (CC) Dave King/©DK Images; **2** Dave King/©DK Images; **5** (T) ©Corbis/Jupiter Images; **6** (TC) Dusk/Fotolia, (BL) Kavita/Fotolia, (Inset) Popperfoto/Getty Images; **8** ©Victor Leonidovich/Shutterstock; **9** (TR) ©OJO Images Ltd/Alamy; **10** (C) ©Robyn Mackenzie/Shutterstock; **12** Carlos Davilla/Getty Images; **18** ©Indeed/Getty Images; **20** (TR) Joe Blossom/Alamy; **21** (CR) ©Davis Barber/PhotoEdit, Inc.; **23** (C) ©Getty Images/Jupiter Images; **25** (CR) ©Radius Images/Alamy; **26** (T, B) Jupiter Images;

30 (C) ©Image Source , (Bkgrd) NASA; **31** (BL) ©Davis Barber/PhotoEdit, Inc., (CL) ©Indeed/Getty Images; **32** (TR) ©Radius Images/Alamy; **35** (BCL) © Joe Blossom/Alamy, (B) Dave King/©DK Images; **36** (BC) ©TongRo Image Stock/Alamy, (TC, CL) Jupiter Images; **38** ©Lisette Le Bon/SuperStock; **41** (TR) Andy Crawford/©DK Images; **43** (CR) Jupiter Images; **44** (BC) ©SSPL/Getty Images, (BL) DK Images, (CL) Jupiter Images, (BR) U.S. Army Photo; **45** (TR) ©Adam Gault/Getty Images; **46** (BR) ©George Rose/Getty Images; **48** (Bkgrd) ©Jupiterimages/Thinkstock, (CC) ©PaulPaladin/Shutterstock, (CR) Corbis; **49** (BL) Getty Images; **51** (CR) ©Masterfile Royalty-Free, (BR) ©Tom & Pat Leeson/Photo Researchers, Inc., (TCL) Getty Images; **52** ©Kim Karpeles/Alamy Images; **53** (BL) ©Comstock Images/Thinkstock, (BR) ©Comstock/Thinkstock; **54** (T) ©Masterfile Royalty-Free, (C) ©Tim Platt/Getty Images; **58** ©Chris Willson/Alamy Images; **59** (BR) ©Masterfile Royalty-Free, (TL) ©Tom & Pat Leeson/Photo Researchers, Inc., (TR) Jupiter Images; **61** (B) ©Lisette Le Bon/SuperStock; **62** (CR) ©David Davis/Shutterstock, (CL) Getty Images, (TR) Jupiter Images; **71** (BC) ©Eric Gevaert/Shutterstock, (TC) ©photosbyjohn/Shutterstock; **72** ©photosbyjohn/Shutterstock; **75** ©Michael Patrick O'Neill/Alamy Images; **76** (T) Dave King/©DK Images; **78** ©Masterfile Royalty-Free; **80** (T) ©mycola/Shutterstock, (TL) ©Rannev/Shutterstock; **81** (TL) ©Galyna Andrushko/Shutterstock, (CR) Corbis; **82** ©Tony Sweet/Getty Images; **84** ©imagebroker/Alamy Images; **86** (T) ©Visions of America, LLC/Alamy, (B) Jupiter Images; **87** (R) ©Lisa Dearing/Alamy; **88** (C) ©Jerry Whaley/Alamy, (T) ©Lisa Dearing/Alamy; **89** (Inset) ©Eric Gevaert/Alamy, (Bkgrd) ©Wave Royalty Free/Alamy; **90** ©Richard Broadwell/Alamy; **91** (C) ©Daniel Sweeney (escapeimages)/Alamy, (T) ©Steve Hamblin/Alamy, (B) Acorn Studios plc, London/©DK Images; **92** (T) ©Masterfile Royalty-Free; **93** (C) ©Vibe Images/Alamy; **94** ©FloridaStock/Shutterstock; **95** Jupiter Images; **98** (B) ©DEA PICTURE LIBRARY/Getty Images, (TL) ©Jupiterimages/Thinkstock, (TR) ©Warren Photographic/Photo Researchers, Inc.; **99** (TL) ©DEA PICTURE LIBRARY/Getty Images, (BR) ©Joe Tucciarone/Photo Researchers, Inc., (TR) ©Tom Brakefield/Thinkstock, (CR) P. W. Sykes/USFWS; **100** (B) Andy Crawford/Courtesy of the Royal Tyrrell Museum of Palaeontology, Alberta, Canada/©DK Images, (TR) Colin Keates/Courtesy of the Natural History Museum, London/©DK Images; **104** NASA Archive/NASA; **105** (CL) ©imagebroker/Alamy Images, (BL) ©Lisa Dearing/Alamy, (CR) ©Masterfile Royalty-Free, (TL) ©Tony Sweet/Getty Images; **107** (TC) ©FloridaStock/Shutterstock, (TR) ©Lisa Dearing/Alamy, (BR) ©Richard Broadwell/Alamy, (CR) ©Wave Royalty Free/Alamy, (TL) Colin Keates/Courtesy of the Natural History Museum, London/©DK Images, (BC) P. W. Sykes/USFWS; **109** (T) ©mycola/Shutterstock, (B) ©photosbyjohn/Shutterstock; **110** (CR) Digital Vision; **111** (TL) ©fotoandrea/Shutterstock, (TR) Megan Lorenz/Fotolia, (TC) Jupiter Images; **112** ©Eric Gevaert/Shutterstock; **115** (BR) ©Regien Paassen/Shutterstock, (TR) Jupiter Images; **116** (TL) ©Al Mueller/Shutterstock, (TR) ©Iliuta Goean/Shutterstock, (TC) ©Joseph/Shutterstock; **117** (CR) ©Doug Lemke/Shutterstock, (TR) ©Galushko Sergey/Shutterstock, (BR) ©Kat Mack/Shutterstock, (TL) ©Loo Joo Pheng/Shutterstock; **118** ©Sean Russell/Getty Images; **119** (BL) ©Kent Sorensen/Shutterstock, (R) ©Nadezhda Bolotina/Shutterstock, (CR) ©oriontrail/Shutterstock; **120** (TR) ©G-ZStudio/Shutterstock, (C) ©Hagit Berkovich/Shutterstock, (B) ©WaterFrame/Alamy Images; **121** (T) ©IRA/Shutterstock, (BR) ©Ludmila Yilmaz/Shutterstock, (BL) Ingram Publishing/Thinkstock, (BCL) ©Panaglotis Milonas/iStockphoto, (BCR) ©ZTS/Shutterstock, (C) Melinda Fawver/Shutterstock;